The Life, Old Age, and Death of a Working-Class Woman

Didier Eribon is a prominent French sociologist and author on matters of social class, identity, sexuality and rebellion. He is internationally renowned for his biography of Michel Foucault and his groundbreaking memoir *Returning to Reims*.

DIDIER ERIBON

The Life, Old Age, and Death of a Working-Class Woman

Translated by Michael Lucey

PENGUIN BOOKS

PENGUIN BOOKS

UK | USA | Canada | Ireland | Australia
India | New Zealand | South Africa

Penguin Books is part of the Penguin Random House group of companies
whose addresses can be found at global.penguinrandomhouse.com.

Penguin Random House UK
One Embassy Gardens, 8 Viaduct Gardens, London SW11 7BW

penguin.co.uk

Originally published as *Vie, vieillesse et mort d'une femme du peuple*
by Éditions Flammarion, Paris 2023
First published in the United States of America by Semiotext(e) 2024
First published in Great Britain by Allen Lane 2025
Published in Penguin 2026
001

This book is supported by the Institut français (Royaume-Uni)
as part of the Burgess programme

Typeset by Six Red Marbles UK, Thetford, Norfolk
Printed and bound in Great Britain by Clays Ltd, Elcograf S.p.A.

The authorized representative in the EEA is Penguin Random House Ireland,
Morrison Chambers, 32 Nassau Street, Dublin D02 YH68

A CIP catalogue record for this book is available from the British Library

ISBN: 978-1-802-06521-3

Penguin Random House is committed to a sustainable future
for our business, our readers and our planet. This book is made from
Forest Stewardship Council® certified paper.

For G., of course

I

1

I would only go to Fismes twice as it turned out. But there was a moment when it seemed that this town of a few thousand people, thirty kilometers north of Reims, would become, for some months or even years, a regular part of my life.

I told myself that I would find a day to visit the town hall that had only just been completed in 1912 before being completely destroyed in the First World War, and then rebuilt in the mid-1920s in the same late-Renaissance style as before. I imagined I would go for a walk in the area behind that strangely solemn building whose setting is not quite that of a village, nor quite urban, around the marketplace lined with different stores and with tall houses some of which proudly display their art deco ornamentation, similar to houses one finds in the center of Reims, having been built at the same time and under the same circumstances. I pictured myself going into the books-newspapers-stationary gift shop, whose windows offered an odd assortment of items that included the final volumes of Faulkner's *Complete Works*, recently published in the Bibliothèque de la Pléiade, with a poster from the Gallimard publishing house advertising an initial promotional price, set alongside endless how-to and self-help books, travel and restaurant guides, roadmaps, and best-selling paperbacks that caught the eye with their garish covers; perhaps

I would buy a magazine or the regional newspaper for my mother, leaf through it for a moment at the café across the way, where I'd spend an hour or two while she was taking a nap, before taking out the book I had brought with me to read. I imagined walking along the streets that suddenly and without warning turn into country roads; or walking as far as the bridge at Fismette. I had just learned, while I was reading up on the layout and the history of this area, that it had been destroyed in 1918 amid fierce fighting—face-to-face combat with bayonets and flamethrowers—between German troops and a battalion of American soldiers, resulting in a horrifying number of deaths of soldiers on both sides… A new bridge, with columns topped with statues, had been paid for by the Commonwealth of Pennsylvania in 1928 as a memorial—one among many in this region—built in honor of the victims of that insanely bloody time. How could one imagine that the area around this town—now so calm, so peaceful, and where in the afternoons of these summer days a near-total silence reigned, one only occasionally interrupted by the sound of a car, truck, or tractor engine—had been the scene, only a century earlier, of such an explosion of sound and fury, of violence and horror, lasting several years, lasting all the way through the final months, the final days, the final hours of a slaughter that the great Jaurès had sought in vain to prevent, paying with his life for the lucidity and the courage that were the hallmark of his commitments. This memorial bridge had then in its turn been destroyed during the German offensive in 1940 and once again rebuilt in identical form in the 1950s. Here was a monument that I would have to visit; it seemed at the same time so beautiful and so sad in the photographs of it. Would I be able to find documents or works that described in a broader way the history of this large village and its surroundings? I would have to inquire at the bookstore / stationary shop on my next trip.

None of these daydreams would be realized. In some way, Fismes itself will never be anything but a name to me—an ephemeral location in my mental universe. As I said, I only went there twice—on two consecutive days. It was during the month of August… At that point in time, I imagined I would be coming here regularly to see my mother, once my brothers and I had moved her into the nursing home where we had finally managed to find her an "open spot." There was nothing else we could think of to do. We had been speaking with her about it for some time already. At first, we talked about a studio in the wing of a retirement home that was intended for people who were still physically independent. She accepted the plan. One of my brothers went with her so she could see the place and decide if it suited her, having first obtained the approval of the institution's doctor. It was on the edge of a distant suburb, a new one in the process of being constructed, not far from the large, old village of Bezannes, with a beautiful Roman church from the eleventh century. A station had recently been built in the middle of the countryside there to serve as a regional stop for the high-speed train from Paris-Est whose final destination was not Reims, but rather Strasbourg or Luxembourg. The institution's premises, along with a few other buildings that had sprung up out of the ground nearby, were modern but isolated, and made for—or at least they did at this moment—a cold, inhuman setting (something straight out of a Jacques Tati film). My mother said no: "I don't want to live there." Hardly surprising, as far as I was concerned.

My brother, who had done all the footwork, had found all the missing documents, had filled out endless forms (it is unimaginable, until you have to do it, how much paperwork is required in order to get into a nursing home!), and who had taken her for this visit, was furious. I pointed out to him that she was the one who was going to have to live there, and so it was up to her to decide.

Two years later, she changed her mind. She accepted what she had earlier refused. But things were not so simple: the doctor would have once again to give his approval. He saw right away that her health had deteriorated significantly and that, despite her desperate efforts to convince him of the opposite (here she was following the somewhat absurd demands of my brother), in truth she could now only walk with great difficulty. The doctor was the one who said no this time. And in order to be admitted to the other part of the establishment, the one for those who were no longer independent, not only were there other steps to be taken, there also had to be an opening—which there wasn't. We dropped the subject. Or rather, we thought and talked about it endlessly, without ever making a decision. Yet something had to be done! What choice was left? She was no longer able to leave home and could barely get around her own apartment. She had fallen several times at night after getting up to use the bathroom or in the morning when taking a shower. These incidents were becoming more and more serious. One Sunday when I was coming to visit her, I called her as I was leaving the train station. There was no answer. I tried again in the bus to Tinqueux, the place on the outskirts of Reims where she had been living. Having arrived at the entry gate to the courtyard around which the elegant and fairly new public-housing buildings stood, I called on the intercom. Still no response. Finally, some neighbors let me in. I went up to the fourth floor where her apartment was and rang the bell. I heard her call out "Give me five minutes" without coming to open the door. I tried speaking to her through the door: "Open the door! What's going on? Are you OK?" But all she did was repeat, in a strange voice, "Give me five minutes." In the end I said, "If you don't open the door, I'm calling the fire department." "Just give me five minutes." After half an hour, I called the fire department. The door was locked from the inside with the keys in the lock. They couldn't open it; it was too thick, too heavy. They would have had to demolish the entire doorframe. Instead, they used their ladder on the outside wall to reach the balcony, and broke the balcony's glass door to get in. Once inside, they opened the door for me. My mother was lying on the floor. She had fallen and hadn't been able to get back up. She had crawled to the hallway when she heard me ring the bell, but she hadn't been able to lift herself, not even onto her knees in order to reach the key. She was naked. I looked away: to see one's mother naked, one's elderly mother, would have been troubling enough on its own, but to see her sprawled on the floor that way—eyes wandering, as if she were hallucinating—had something unbearable about it. I ran to her room to find some article of clothing to give to one of the firemen who covered her with it.

I called her doctor. The firemen moved her to the sofa and, after some administrative formalities—a report on their intervention that I had to sign if I remember correctly—they left. The doctor arrived two hours later after finishing his visits. He called an ambulance to take her to the hospital. She had been lying on the floor for an extended period of time, and he explained to me that that could have serious consequences for her circulation, her heart, and her general health… I spent the night in a hotel in Reims so that I could visit her the next day. She spent two weeks in the hospital: tests showed some serious inflammation that needed to be brought under control. Then she returned home. The same scene would recur at regular intervals: she would fall during the night or early in the morning and would remain immobilized on the floor… and the nurse who at that point was coming every day to give her her shots or to make sure that she took her pills, and who had a set of keys, would find her when she arrived a few hours later. Unable to lift her up off the floor on her own, she would call the fire department. Finally, the fire department announced that this was not their job and that any time it happened again, they would charge for their services. I learned that there was a name for this: an "emergency lifting fee," with a set rate. I'm in no way being sarcastic, nor am I criticizing anyone. In fact, I'm full of admiration for their dedication and their efficiency. But obviously things could not continue in this manner. At this point in time my brothers began looking for a different nursing home: one that would accept someone who, like my mother, was no longer independent; one that could take her reasonably soon; one that she would agree to go to; and, not insignificantly, one that was economically manageable. That was a lot to ask for. She had often dreamed of moving somewhere near Rochefort, in the southwest of France, where my youngest brother lived with his wife and two children, whom she adored. I joked with her about it: "You want to become one of the 'young girls of Rochefort'!" I don't actually know if she had ever seen Jacques Demy's film, but at least she knew the title and one of its famous songs, sung (or lip-synched rather, because it's not their voices on the soundtrack) by Catherine Deneuve and Françoise Dorléac:

"Nous sommes deux soeurs jumelles, nées sous le signe des Gémeaux..." (Here we are, twin sisters, and born Geminis too ...). She would laugh: "Don't be silly!" It must be said that my brother was not too enthusiastic about the idea, and he let her know that, as busy as he was with work, he would scarcely have time to come see her and even less time to take care of her... As for her grandchildren, my mother nourished certain illusions about the affection that they felt for her: to be taken to visit her was a chore that they agreed to as rarely as possible. Nothing explicit was said, but little by little the idea faded on its own. My older brother, who lives in Belgium, near Charleroi, with his partner, invited her to come live with them. For her, that was out of the question: there were too many comings and goings in their house—the sons and daughters of my brother's partner with their children and their dogs, which meant lots of noise, too much noise... She would never be able to put up with living in such surroundings. One time after visiting them, she couldn't stop saying how depressing she had found that part of the country. "It's really ugly, where they live," she explained to me, among other more personal reasons. What I took her to be saying was that as someone who had struggled so hard to escape from poor neighborhoods, from working-class areas, she had no desire to find herself back in the "projects," in one of the working-class neighborhoods on the outskirts of the cities of the Walloon Region. They were identical to those found in the north of France, with their rows of small houses, depressingly identical, one next to the other, that today house the precariat of our deindustrialized era after having housed mine workers or factory workers. Zola had set the scene of his unforgettable novel *Germinal* here. I suggested that she could find a retirement community somewhere in the area around Paris.

Forgetting her unfulfilled desire to move to Rochefort, she stubbornly refused to consider it, giving as a reason both strange and unanswerable "No, Reims is where I belong." I persisted: "If you were in Paris or nearby, I could visit you more often." I could already imagine it to myself. There is a retirement home not far from where I live whose white exterior is a bit dirty and looks like it hasn't been repainted in a while, but whose reception area, from the outside looking in, looks quite welcoming. There's a scene that I often observe from day to day on the terrace of the café on the corner of that street when the weather is nice: an elderly person, almost always a woman, is seated at a table, a cane balanced on the edge of her chair, with, across from her, a younger person, someone from the next generation, a man or a woman, most likely her son or daughter. It's easy to see who they are: a resident of the home who is still somewhat independent, who can still walk the few dozen yards from the home with one of their children, to have a glass of juice or a cup of tea and enjoy the sunshine. I couldn't help seeing myself seated at a table on the terrace, or in some similar situation in a different neighborhood, with my mother to whom I would be paying a visit, and would have proposed the short walk to the café next door so that she could enjoy the good weather that afternoon and spend a few minutes experiencing once more the daily life and activity of the city.

But she was stubborn: "No, Reims is where I live." Was she afraid of being even more isolated in Paris than she was in Reims, cut off from the few connections she still had left, after the deaths of so many people around her, or after all the quarrels she had provoked, notably with my father's sisters, whom, in one of those moments of anger that were typical of her, she had insulted and accused of all sorts of petty wrongs, and who were no longer interested in having anything to do with her? And then, the truth was that she was hopelessly in love, and the idea of no longer being able to see the man she was crazy about, obsessed with, was unbearable to her. (I'll come back to this.) If she couldn't be near her grandchildren in Rochefort, she wanted to stay close to the person with whom she had been so happy these last few years. In any case, in Paris things would have been complicated because, it turns out, waiting lists for those establishments were apparently long and, on top of that, the rates were unaffordable: well beyond her means and well beyond our collective means. Perhaps I could have found a less expensive establishment in the suburbs, but, given that she didn't want to change regions, there didn't seem any point in my undertaking a more thorough search for such a place. So it would have to be Reims, or else nearby. Reims itself seemed highly unlikely: prospects were scarce, my brother told me, after making a few inquiries, with waiting lists extending to two or three years. That's why it would be Fismes in the end, the EHPAD in Fismes. A former hospital that had been renovated, it had in front a handsome building of white stone and red bricks with a little turret on top, and then behind that, on either side of a grassy courtyard, modern buildings that had only recently been completed.

EHPAD is the acronym currently used to designate an *établissement pour l'hébergement des personned âgées dépendantes*, an "institution for the accommodation of elderly people in need of care," which is to say a nursing home in which medical supervision is provided. My mother had clearly become an "elderly person in need of care." And her state of health was such that she needed constant medical attention.

2

I had promised my mother I would be there on the day that she was admitted to the home. To get to Fismes, I had to take the train from Paris to Reims; I don't have a car, and I've never even obtained a driver's license, something, as I've often noticed, that is common among gay men living in Paris—"the same causes producing the same effects," as one of my female friends had jokingly observed, pointing out that none of the gay Parisian men she knew actually knew how to drive. With the high-speed train, the journey has become a fairly quick one: forty-five minutes. Before that, when I first moved to Paris, it was much longer. It took an hour and a half, but during the second half of the journey it was easier to enjoy the scenery, the well-known hillsides of the champagne vineyards and the villages of the wine-making region. After that, because the regional train service out of Reims had been suspended for the summer, I took the RTA bus, the Régie des transports de l'Aisne, the company that provided service between Reims and Soissons. It made multiple stops, including one at Fismes. There I met my brother (the younger one), who had rented a car, and my mother in front of the nursing home that she would be living in from then on.

I arrived first. They arrived fifteen minutes later. When the car my brother was driving passed through the gate to the courtyard and stopped in front of the reception office, my mother lowered the window to say hello to me; she was weeping. She was distraught and could barely manage to talk between her sobs. It felt like my heart was breaking. What were we doing to her?

My brother had packed into the car everything that it was necessary or important for her to keep: there were her clothes, of course, and then her television with its DVD player, her radio with its CD player, a few books and piles of magazines, two huge boxes of photographs, framed reproductions of paintings that we would hang on her walls… We wanted her to feel at home because, as we would be saying to her over and over again, this was her home now, this was where she would be at home. She would respond to us uttering resigned protests that began with: "No, it will never be my home," then "I'll never be at home here," until she would grow tired of what must have seemed to her our inability to understand her: "Yes, I know, but it's not the same."

Some nurse's aides put my mother in a wheelchair and took her to her room, which we saw for the first time along with her. As in the past, it had been a different brother, the one from Rochefort, the youngest of the four, who had come a while earlier to visit the place. He had found it to be quite nice. The administration had told him that we would probably have to wait a few months before a room would "open up." We had thought that seemed like rather a long wait, without considering too carefully what a shorter wait would have meant: another person's rapid demise. But at least the interval would allow my mother to prepare herself mentally for this huge and irreversible change in her life. Then a few weeks later he received a call: a room had "opened up" earlier than they had foreseen. If we wanted it, we had to take it right away. We were not the only ones on the waiting list, far from it! Everything happened in a rush. My mother was not yet ready to move. Would she have been a few months later? I'm not sure. First, she said that she had changed her mind, and that she no longer wanted to leave her own home. She reacted out of fear or out of panic in the face of a decision that was as impossible for her as it was necessary—necessary both for her and for us. But what could we reply to her? It was her decision, of course. And yet some solution had to be found; she could no longer live alone. We once again began the same discussion. "Be reasonable, there's really no other choice," I insisted, as if an argument based on "reason" made any sense in the face of this wave of anxiety that was not in itself unreasonable and certainly not irrational. She replied: "Of course I know that, but still, you have to understand… "

Of course I understood! Only too well. But it was necessary to "be reasonable." And in the end, she said, in resignation: "Yes, I have to be reasonable."

These horrific sentences, articulating so simply the necessity of giving way to the inevitable, haunt me even today. Memories came back to me of my fevered reading of Descartes when I was a philosophy student, and of the absolute refusal provoked in me, still deeply marked as I was at that point by my youthful Marxism, by his affirmation of a moral stoicism that I perceived as an abandonment of politics and of the possibility for action. I easily found the volume of his works on my bookshelf, many pages covered with annotations, many paragraphs underlined, notably this one, one of the most famous, of course, from the *Discourse on the Method*: "My third maxim was to try always to master myself rather than fortune, and change my desires rather than the order of the world. In general I would become accustomed to believing that nothing lies entirely within our power except our thoughts, so that after doing our best in dealing with matters external to us, whatever we fail to achieve is absolutely impossible so far as we are concerned."

That being the case, "making a virtue of necessity, as they say, we shall not desire to be healthy when ill or free when imprisoned, any more than we now desire to have bodies of a material as indestructible as diamond or wings to fly like the birds."[1]

Here I was listening to myself offer my mother an extremely simplified version of the "maxim" that I had found so offensive years before, as if I now fully appreciated its wisdom, its pertinence, even its implacable self-evidence in certain situations such as the one in which we now found ourselves. Her "illness" was old age, the nursing home would be her "prison," and it was her duty to give up desiring to be healthy, to be able to move freely, and to make her own choices, because she was no longer capable of any of those things and never would be again.

The order of the world—in this particular instance, the inevitability of growing old, the physical consequences of the harsh conditions of working-class jobs and the general conditions of life associated with them, the reality of contemporary family forms, the history of urban planning and public housing, the political and social management of old age, illness, and assisted living, etc., everything that makes up the past and the present of a society—found itself condensed into this fateful moment in which an unavoidable decision was forced upon us, forced upon her, pitilessly sweeping aside her wishes, her desires, and any possibility of resistance or action. We see here how heavy the weight of the social and historical determinisms that underlie a simple conversation between two people can be. She had to accept what had become inevitable, and the only way her protests could express themselves was through tears. I knew all too well the limits placed on anyone's will, on the faculty to decide, on the capacity to act: they are inscribed in each of us by all that defines us, by what I have called "social verdicts." I knew them well; they were perfectly familiar to me; I had not only experienced them in my life, all throughout my life, as everyone does, but I had also described them, decoded them, analyzed them in each of my books. But there is always a certain amount of "give" in the mechanisms that constrain us, there is always a space, however tiny, however hemmed in by forms of structural inertia, for individual or collective transformation. However powerful may be the limitations posed on our desires—beginning with the way those desires are restrictively delimited in the form of aspirations that have been conditioned and shaped by our social affiliations or origins (taken in the widest sense), by our class, gender, race, etc., and by the volume of "capital" (economic, cultural, social) that any of us possesses (or lacks)—it is nonetheless the case that the power of these determinisms and these forms of determination is never absolute. That should go without saying. Those who imagine that they are critiquing "determinist" forms of thought by offering this obvious truth as an objection to it are naively overlooking the reality both of global transformations that are social and historical in nature and of the collective and individual trajectories that take place within these general frameworks and in the course of which change and permanence, or constraint and freedom, are always tightly imbricated with each other, linked together, combined in different ways, or accentuated differently according to various circumstances and individuals. And yet, in these conversations with my mother, I was forced to realize that age and physical weakness constitute frameworks, chains, "prisons" that reduce to nothingness anything that had been left of the power to run from fate, to escape to some degree or other: yes, you could wish to, but no, you would not be able to. And in the end, you would no longer wish to because you were no longer able to.

In Shichirô Fukazawa's short story "Narayama," which takes place in a Japanese village in the 1860s, people who are seventy years old have to leave for the mountain, where they will await death; that is to say, they have to withdraw to a place that they will never leave, from which they will never return. Their eldest sons take them there, carrying them attached to their backs on planks to which they cling or to which they are attached. Some of them consent willingly or are simply resigned to it: to go and die on the mountain is the last step in the normal course of life. Others rebel against it, and must be forced to go, sometimes by means of violence. It is important to emphasize that the book should not be read as some kind of historical or ethnographic reconstruction: it is a work of fiction, not some kind of realistic description.[2] It can nonetheless function as a kind of parable. This imaginative work (adapted for film first by Keisuke Kinoshita and later by Shôhei Imamura[3]) offers an allegorical vision of the social (as well as physical) relegation that lies in wait for the elderly and the two possible attitudes of those subjected to it: follow the rule, submit to it voluntarily, prepare yourself for it, or else refuse it, attempt to evade it, to escape from it—before finally being captured by it and by those whose job it is to enforce it. Doubtless there is a middle term or a continuum of attitudes between these two opposing poles: resignation mixed with reflexes of revolt; or the inverse, a stubborn refusal that fades over time, eroded by the undeniable evidence of growing difficulties with mobility, and that transforms itself little by little, by way of many hesitations and prevarications, into a barely formulated, hesitant acquiescence marked by sadness and depression...

The age of departure has been delayed, of course, and a car has replaced the wooden plank; it is no longer the oldest son who is driving, and yet I can insert my mother and her sons (myself included) into a tableau that is analogous to the imaginary and symbolical construction that we find in Japanese literature. The nursing home in Fismes becomes the mountain of Narayama, and my mother takes on one by one or all at once the different attitudes of the elderly people (refusal and protest; acceptance or resignation and submission...), just as we took on the different roles of the son: to act as if this were written, prescribed, inevitable because it was part of the natural order of things, the way one generation followed another (and here I remember the expression my great-grandmother would use fatalistically, when I was still a child and unable to understand its full meaning, *C'est la roue qui tourne*, "The wheel never stops turning"), to convince her that she had to give in to the way the world was, and consequently to force her, by way of rational arguments and repeated attempts at persuasion, to comply—acts of soft violence, of course, yet which she still experienced as extremely violent. She was being sentenced to a loss of freedom. And now her opinion barely mattered; maybe she had avoided this for a few years, then a few months, then a few weeks, delaying the day that she would be admitted to the nursing home, but she hadn't been able to prevent the inevitable outcome.

And so here we were! From the window you could see a few meters of lawn leading up to a wall. Beyond this wall, which surrounded the buildings and courtyards that made up the nursing home, you could see a more or less rural landscape, with small houses, a road, trees, fields… Taken all together it was a fairly agreeable view, assuming you were someone capable of going out for a walk or at least standing up and gazing off into the distance. But what about for her, someone who would soon be capable of neither of those things?

To create some kind of a resemblance, however faint, to the apartment she had just been forced to leave, we had hung framed photos on the walls, and some reproductions of paintings that she had had at home (country landscapes and seascapes, so characteristic of the decorative tastes of the working class). We had positioned the television screen (it was too big for this room) facing the bed and the CD player next to it; then we filled the wardrobe with the clothes and other miscellaneous belongings that my brother had packed in a large suitcase. He couldn't stop grumbling and making odd observations such as "I shouldn't be here hanging clothes in a closet; that's women's work." I sighed, thinking to myself, "What an asshole," but otherwise chose not to react… The situation was painful enough without adding to it an argument with him. Still, it was dismaying to rediscover how strange and unbearable a family "bond" could be. What did I have in common with him? Nothing. Absolutely nothing. Except that we were both there because we had to be, to take care of our mother. We occupied ourselves around her. She was there lying on the bed, surely worrying to herself about what her life was going to be like, assigned this room to live in, on the third floor of this building, cut off from the external world. She seemed exhausted, stunned by the emotions that besieged and overwhelmed her.

My brother went back to Reims to be with his wife and children (they had arrived a few days earlier from Réunion, where they live) in the apartment that my mother had just left and where the furniture had yet to be removed. I was relieved when he left. I'd had enough of listening to his foolishness. I said: "Goodbye. See you later." He replied, sarcastically: "You mean in thirty years?" And he was right. I hadn't seen him in thirty years and, as it turns out, I haven't seen him since. I stayed with my mother, just the two of us, until the end of the afternoon when I had to take the last bus back to Reims. I was discovering the inconveniences of an institution like this one, situated so far out of town. I had to be mindful of the public transport schedules, and they stopped quite early. There were no hotels in Fismes. I had made some inquiries, looking ahead to future visits: there had been a hotel-restaurant with a few rooms close to the nursing home, but it had stopped taking overnight guests six months earlier. In any case, I had been planning to spend the night in Reims. I wanted to take advantage of this short stay to revisit the cathedral with its legendary statues—the *Smiling Angel*—its Treasury with its precious objects (the robes and jewels from royal coronations), the Knoebel stained glass windows that were installed in the 1990s, the older ones by Chagall, from the 1960s. (The son of the master glassworker who had constructed them was in the same class with me in my last three years of high school, and I had been deeply impressed, and even a little unsettled, on the day when he had invited me and a few other classmates to the handsome bourgeois house in the center of town where he lived with his parents, and had shown us the celebrated artist's book of sketches. He obviously belonged to a different world from mine; the world of my family was one from which art was totally absent and where no one knew who Chagall was.)

On the road back, we again passed through places I had come to know well: Muizon, where my mother and father had lived for twenty years; other towns and villages, separated by fields; countryside or semirural areas; industrial zones where factories of different sizes and warehouses of well-known brands sat next to each other; then Tinqueux, just outside Reims, where my mother had lived for the past three or four years after a short stay of a few months in Reims proper, in public housing that had been built behind the central station. She had moved there when she had had to leave the house in Muizon, but hadn't wanted to remain there because she couldn't stand either the noise made by teenagers in the street or the continuous sound of the cars coming and going during the night from the garage that was just underneath her windows (and, as someone who likes nothing so much as peace and quiet, I fully understood how unpleasant that must have been for her). But even more significantly for her, she couldn't stand how many "foreigners" there were living in this new neighborhood. Arguing with her about this was pointless, since she ended every effort to talk about it with sentences like "I don't like this area; it doesn't even feel like France here." What could you say to her? She wanted to move again, and so move she did. She felt at home in Tinqueux, even if she was sad that she hadn't been able to return to Muizon, a large village that she had really enjoyed and would often talk about nostalgically. But for her to have been able to live there, she would have needed to be allocated a unit on a single level. She could no longer handle a flight of stairs like the one in the two-story house she had lived in earlier, the one whose description opens *Returning to Reims.* In fact, that is why she had had to leave. But there were no units of that kind. Or none were available. There were some under construction, they had told her at the town hall. But they wouldn't be ready for some time. Time, however, was not something she had: she was in a hurry to leave the place where she felt so uncomfortable every time she had to go out or even simply every time she opened her window. That is how she ended up in Tinqueux, because that's what the housing authority had offered her. She had liked it there, and so that put an end to the short stopover in Reims that was part of her post-Muizon peregrination: to her it felt like a return to France, a homecoming, after those few months spent above a garage in a foreign country. It was a fourth-floor apartment, but with an elevator that was modern and convenient. Then later, when she could no longer live alone in Tinqueux, it was Fismes and the nursing home, because it had to be: another exile, certainly, another "foreign" country, even if of a much different kind of foreignness, and one that she would have to get used to, because this time she would not be able to say that she didn't like it here and wanted to leave. There would be no further move. I found myself asking myself, almost against my will and while trying to chase these thoughts away, how much time she had left, how much time she would be spending in the home, in that room… and consequently for how long I would be visiting her in the village to which we had just moved her. I was thinking in terms of years. Would she find the means, the energy, the strength to settle in well? How would her time be organized; how would her days unfold in this confined space where she would henceforth—there was no way to deny it—be more or less shut in? I would have to come and see her as often as possible, so that she wouldn't be too lonely. I was preparing myself for this mentally, thinking about what was to come: "Once a month won't be enough; once a week would be ideal, but hard to sustain…" I didn't find this idea unpleasant: I had enjoyed those short trips when I would go to see her in Muizon or in Tinqueux in the recent past, the train to Reims, where I would spend two or three nights, the city with the streets and squares that I remembered from my past, its monuments, its cafés and restaurants. I showed all these places to Geoffroy, my partner, when he was able to come with me: the Foujita Chapel, the art deco buildings, the Saint-Remi Basilica, the traditional brasseries that were located around the Boulingrin marketplace—and the champagne bars throughout the area, for a night when cheering up was needed after a particularly depressing afternoon with my mother. It would be exactly the same for the upcoming trips to Fismes. For me, all that would have changed was the name of the town where she lived. Whereas for her, all of life would have been turned upside down.

I looked out the windows of the bus during the whole trip. So many questions without answers, so many images from the past and the present, so many doubts were passing through my mind, jostling each other. I didn't know what to think. I was perplexed and sad. I told myself I should reread Simone de Beauvoir's *Old Age* and Norbert Elias's *The Loneliness of the Dying* to come to a better understanding of the situation and to come up with a better way of reacting to it.[4]

The route ended in a square that served as a kind of bus station, a few dozen meters behind the cathedral. To gaze over at the chevet of Notre-Dame de Reims in the setting sun: what an imposing scene for such a gloomy moment!

As I left, I had said to her: "I'll be back tomorrow." And the next day I went back the same way, by bus, from Reims to Fismes, to spend the afternoon with her. I opened the boxes of photos that my brother had brought the day before. He had pointed them out to me with the following words, uttered in a tone that I perceived, perhaps wrongly, as somewhat hostile or, at the least, as scornful: "Here's a gold mine for you, for your next book." I took the photos out of the boxes—of course I had never seen them—and showed them to my mother. She commented on them: "That's me and your dad on a trip to Turkey," "In this one we're in Tunisia." They were tours, organized by the workers' council of the factory where my father was working or had worked (since they were able to take advantage of these opportunities even after he retired). In many of the snapshots you see them on group outings to restaurants in the evening. These organized trips always included, along with various tourist outings, a dinner in a restaurant with entertainment and musicians. It was on one of these trips, in Andalusia, when they were in Grenada, that a Romani guitarist had said to my mother: "You are one of us, I can tell." She knew that it was true, too, since she had always spoken of her Romani heritage with some pride, despite otherwise being quite racist.

The hours passed. It was time for me to go; once again the bus timetables were what they were! I promised her I would be back soon. I felt guilty. I had plans to spend two weeks on vacation in Italy. The reservations had been made a while back, when I thought that she wouldn't be moving into the nursing home for a few more months. It was difficult to cancel the reservations, especially since I wasn't traveling alone.

But of course I'd come see her again as soon as I got back…

3

On the day after my mother's arrival at the nursing home, while I was in her room with her, someone knocked on the door: a woman I had never seen before came in, and not only was my mother not surprised by this visit, she seemed pleased by it. When the woman left, I asked her who that person was, someone she had just spoken with for at least half an hour and obviously knew quite well.

It was an old friend of hers. "That's Yoyo," she said, using again the diminutive form of her first name that she had used in greeting her ("Oh, Yoyo, it's you!"). The woman's husband had been living in the nursing home for several months now. My mother knew this (how?), and she had managed to go visit with him a few hours earlier in his room, which he never left, and which wasn't far from hers. This resident of the nursing home was someone who had worked in the same factory as my father for a number of years. Both before and after retiring, he and his wife, like my father and mother, would make a point of going on the vacation trips organized by the enterprise's workers council. In a few of the photographs that I found in the boxes my brother had brought, my father could be seen singing, holding a microphone in his hand, or wearing a cap and a scarf around his neck as a kind of costume, or a veil over his face (in Morocco? in

Tunisia?). "He was always clowning it up," my mother remarked. Indeed, he had always enjoyed standing out, being noticed, the one to tell the jokes, the live wire on festive evenings... My mother hated all that, and disliked him for it, but that is who he was and who he had always been. She would stay in the background, with Yolande and perhaps a few of the other women. I wish I could have found a few photos of those women together: group portraits that would have shown me one of the moments in which my mother might have felt at ease or even a little free. If such photographs exist, I haven't found them. More than that, I would have loved to hear a recording of their conversations, something that obviously doesn't exist: What topics interested them? What did they think about what was going on around them? About the world they lived in?

It was in these recurring circumstances that my mother and Yolande had grown to be fond of each other. There probably weren't many other occasions for them to meet, since in working-class environments friends don't really pay visits to each other and apartments and houses are more often than not considered private spaces, protected from outside glances as much as possible. I never saw my mother invite a friend over—did she even have any?—when we were living in an apartment in a public housing complex, during my childhood and my adolescence. And while I know that there was a woman who lived across from her in Muizon and came over for coffee from time to time, that was much later and after my father's death. I believe that to have been the extent of her friendships. It's hardly necessary to say—it so clearly goes without saying—that if my mother didn't have any women friends, or only a few, she didn't have, and couldn't have had, any male friends either. My mother could never have sat down at a table with a man to talk with him, even less could she have danced with him. That would have provoked a huge scene from my father, including shouting and threats (directed at her and at the man in question); maybe he would even have shoved the table violently and knocked over the chairs. His obsessive jealousy and his frenzied impulses to control my mother meant that he lost control of himself in situations like these. I'm not exaggerating. I saw such a scene with my own eyes when I was very young. During an evening of dancing that followed a long family lunch after someone's wedding, my mother danced a slow dance with one of the men there. My father flew into a state of extreme fury, shoved them apart and screamed at them; he pushed away his own brothers and sisters who were trying to calm him down. I never again saw my mother dance after that incident. She had to be cautious. All it took, in fact, was for my mother to say hello to a man she knew, or for my father to imagine that she had glanced at a man she didn't know, while they were walking down the street for him to become violent.

These group tours of several days each thus served my mother and the other women who took part in them as regular occasions to meet up, and they were important to them because of that. Friendship has many forms, after all, and this form was as good as many others: the friends you went on excursions with. The women got along well and, by all accounts, were quite fond of each other.

Even though they hadn't seen each other in quite a long time, their conversation picked up again as if they had last seen each other just the day before, and soon they had turned to talking about the resentment and even the hatred (the word is certainly not too strong, given what I heard that day) that they felt toward their husbands: my father, who had died more than ten years earlier, and the husband of Yolande, debilitated physically and mentally, living in his room at the nursing home, on a nearby corridor. "He begged me to take him back home, but there was no way I was doing that! I don't want anything more to do with him!" exclaimed my mother's visitor. Then came the litany of reproaches and complaints: both hers and my mother's, one following another or all mixed together, one on top of another... They had never been happy with their spouses, or only right at the very beginning, a long time ago, so long ago that all that followed had obliterated any trace of what they had briefly experienced back in the day. My mother had felt a certain amount of relief when my father died, not only because of the way the Alzheimer's that he had suffered from for several years along with his permanent move to a specialized facility where she went to visit him every day had been a heavy, endless burden for someone who didn't love him, but also because, for the first time since her marriage at the age of twenty, she was alone and free, with no one to be accountable to for what she did or said or thought or looked at... For a time she was able to enjoy this rediscovered autonomy, before new impediments to her freedom of movement caught up with her, those tied to her age and physical decline. Listening to them speak, I had the strong impression that the woman visiting her had welcomed her husband's move to the nursing home with similar feelings: free at last!

In one of her autobiographical works, *What Is Africa to Me?*, Maryse Condé describes how, when visiting Dahomey (Benin today) in the 1960s with two African American tourists she had met on the plane, she spent an evening in a bar with the two women where, after a few drinks, they grew "maudlin" and began to complain about their husbands or partners: "each of us ranted and raved about our partners and shared a string of grievances.... We concluded with a common interrogation: Why do men spoil the lives of women?" One of the women participating in the discussion makes the observations more precise: "'Black men,' specified Maya ... 'It's all because of the way they have been educated. Their mothers, their sisters and society in general treat them like gods—they can do anything they like.'"[5]

The stories Condé tells of the relations that she had with a series of men (Black men) are full of anecdotes and lessons about the ways (not very respectful ones) in which heterosexual men conduct themselves with women. They take up a good portion of her book.

Having listened to the litany of "complaints" uttered in exasperated and vindictive tones by my mother and her friend, which picked up momentum as the conversation went along, I said to myself that, *mutatis mutandis*, the social and cultural laws of masculine domination and the effects they produce in the lives of women don't work all that differently in the world of white people: there too, men often "spoil" the lives of their spouses or partners.

Someone might object that it is not all that rare for couples made up of a man and a woman to continue loving each other for their whole lives, just as it can happen for couples of the same sex. Who would deny it? Still, obviously, it needn't always be the case. Far from it.[6]

And what I am reconstructing here of a conversation overheard in a room in a nursing home between two women who hadn't seen each other in years (and who, in this moment of being reunited, with so much to say to each other, speaking quickly, speaking loudly, as if to make up for lost time, seemed to have forgotten that I was there) would seem to confirm Maryse Condé's observations: when women get together, they complain about the men they live with or have lived with, or they disparage them or make fun of them. They do so in the way Bourdieu wrote about when he reconstructed the general system of relations between the sexes and of masculine domination in Kabylia, which can count as another version of the same phenomenon of reaction—a form of both recognition and resistance—to being in the structurally dominated position.

Even when nothing remains of the past, when everything has disappeared into forgetfulness, still the ineradicable marks of subjection remain.

Yasushi Inoue has written about his mother that as she aged the only things that seemed to stay with her were "painful episodes" from her married life. At a moment when her cognitive decline is already well under way, she launches into a stream of acrimonious memories related to her deceased husband. He writes that despite her usual memory lapses, she exhibits "fragments of the hardships she had suffered because of Father." His conclusion is that his father was "the persecutor" and his mother the "victim."[7]

It often happened, my mother told me during my visit, that on those nights that were among the high points of the group tours, my father and Yolande's husband would disappear together for a certain length of time. "Where did they go?" I asked. "Oh, they went off with women," my mother replied in a tone so harsh that I preferred not to pursue the matter, even though I wasn't totally sure of the exact meaning to give to the words "went off with women" in that particular context.

I did ask her: "But if you all hated your husbands so much, why didn't you get divorced?" The answer she gave was the same one she had given me a few years earlier: "Well, you know, things weren't the same back then as today. It wasn't easy for a woman. Men could do what they wanted, but not women." Certainly, there were many moments when she wanted to. She even took the first few official steps once when my older brother and I were still children. I remember that she took us with her to the police station. (I'm not sure exactly when this was, nor what the circumstances were, but she had told me, when I inquired after we had "reconnected" and I was writing *Returning to Reims*, that the police officer she dealt with had turned her away in no uncertain terms, demonstrating thereby the solidarity of men with each other, and even a kind of spontaneous complicity between men whose behaviors must have been more or less identical.) I also remember that we went with her to the courthouse where she had a meeting with a judge. Why did she give up on this? "He would have caused all sorts of trouble; he would never have left me alone. He would have been outside my place every night raising a ruckus," she told me. I know she wasn't exaggerating. That is indeed what probably would have happened. I could visualize the scene (similar to the violent fights that regularly broke out between them in the different apartments we had lived in, during which my father literally seemed to go crazy, smashing furniture and breaking down doors whenever my mother would flee to another room and lock herself in). There would be the usual mix of pleas, promises, and threats… How far would it have gone? Who knows, and I'd rather not speculate about what he might or might not have done. The worst is never a foregone conclusion, but it always lurks on the horizon. How many women are pursued, harassed, beaten by their husbands or partners while they are deciding to leave them—and even worse, when they courageously manage to do it, and still worse if they get together with another man? Or even worse still, how many women die each year, beaten by a man they no longer wish to live with? The notion of "femicide" has recently been put forward in order to call attention to the fact that this horrific reality is not a sum of individual cases, but rather the final consequence of a system of domination that is both global and an everyday reality.[8] Of course I am not saying that that is what would have happened if my mother had left. I don't see my father, even in the moments where he lost control of himself, becoming her murderer. But when I was a child, I was always aware that if my mother stayed with this man—my father—whom she did not love, it was in large part because she was afraid. She was afraid of the future and she was afraid of him. The fact remains that she did not leave. How was it that she convinced herself not to try to change her life? Or rather, how did the scale of the problems of all kinds she would have had to confront in order to live on her own, or her resignation faced with the sad destiny that she perceived as being hers, manage to convince her not to try to escape from this situation by any means possible?

Édouard Louis has written about how his mother, in a contrary manner, tired of being abused, humiliated, treated as if she were a domestic slave, decided one day to leave behind all these kinds of relationships, as painful as they are destructive, and chose to reinvent her life and carve out a certain amount of freedom from the state of necessity in which she had been imprisoned up until then. The title of his book expresses this situation aptly: *A Woman's Battles and Transformations.*[9]

My mother, who at the time was a housecleaner, had given up in the face of the hardships she would have had to confront had she decided to move out: How to cope with living alone with two children (we were under the age of ten)? How to leave everything behind, find an apartment, earn enough money each month to pay the rent and buy everything else we needed? "How would I have done it?" she repeated over and over during our conversation about this, as if trying to persuade herself that there was no reason to regret the decision she had made at the time, even if it was obvious that she couldn't help dreaming about what her life might have been had she followed through with these plans. Why didn't she return to the idea later? She had two more children, born eight and fourteen years after me, which amounted to a prolongation of her dependent situation. On top of that, she worried about having to start from scratch: "We had worked hard to get a little ahead," by which she meant certain material comforts they had wanted for a long time: a dining room table and a varnished wood buffet, a couch in imitation leather, a Formica kitchen, the television, and so on. "If I'd left, I'd have lost everything." She had been abandoned as a child and raised in an orphanage; then, barely out of childhood, she started work cleaning houses. She didn't want to fall back into such precarious, lonely, and impoverished situations. Did she take a long time making up her mind? Certainly, every day that went by meant her choice to stay was more difficult to change. Life continued its course. Things were what they were! Still, I asked myself this question: Was she always afraid? It might be possible to think that the risk of violence diminished over time. This would be a mistake. There is no particular age at which femicide happens. Quite recently in my neighborhood in Paris I saw small posters on the walls listing the names of women and their ages—seventy-one, seventy-two—followed by this simple annotation: "Killed by her former partner."

I was left perplexed by this conversation between my mother and her friend: What kind of an institution is matrimony, marriage, a lasting relationship that is officially recognized; what kinds of frameworks are these that people enter into at such a young age (at least at that time: my father was twenty-one, my mother was twenty, and by the age of twenty-three she already had two children, which is to say that she lost her freedom very early on), and with the idea that they are permanent? Marriage is a past that lasts a long time: my parents got married in 1950; my father died on December 31, 2005, which was fifty-five years later. I never saw them in love; I never even saw them appreciate each other (nor, at least from my mother's point of view, did I see any respect in her for the person with whom she shared her life and her bed, since, as strange as it may seem, they slept in the same bed).[10]

At the moment they were married, they had, of course, followed all the ceremonial rituals that it would never have crossed their minds to defy. To the contrary: it would seem that one of the things about marriage that is so attractive is precisely the observance of those rituals, and all the ceremonies that accompany them. I have in front of me the "official" photograph (which is to say the one taken by a photographer whose profession—whose way of making a living—is being present in spaces and circumstances like these) intended to immortalize the day: my mother is posed in a long white dress and my father in a grey suit, with a tie, a pocket handkerchief, and a pair of black gloves in his hand… They were, I believe, married in a church, despite being (as were both his family and hers) nonbelievers!

I remember that my father called my mother "dear" and "darling," but these were just words he was in the habit of using, devoid of any feeling (or else they had lost any of the feelings that perhaps colored them at the beginning of their relationship); my mother never called my father "dear," never had a nice thing to say to him, nor a kind gesture for him. The most she did was to use the nickname "Néné" for René when she would call to him or was speaking to him in a family context. It can be difficult or even strange to call someone you live with by their full first name, which explains the use of nicknames or surnames or pet names. Generally speaking and almost without exception, the tone with which she addressed him made obvious the hostile distance that existed between them (especially toward him from her), and that had been in place for such a long time that it had become their daily manner, their way of life. I could put it this way: my mother was unhappy her whole life.

4

As I was leaving, at the end of her second day in the nursing home, as I was telling her we would see each other next month, I found myself clumsily mouthing these absurd sentences: "Don't worry. They'll take good care of you here. You'll see, you'll be happy here."

Today, I am ashamed to have uttered these clichés. My shame was only deepened when I discovered, a few months after my mother's death, a powerful song by Jean Ferrat whose title is precisely that: "Tu verras, tu seras bien" (You'll see, you'll be happy here). The song is made up of a series of phrases addressed to someone who is being admitted, or who will soon be admitted, to some kind of "home." These days, I hear each word he sings as a reproach personally directed at me.

I've already talked about Jean Ferrat, a popular singer affiliated with the Communist Party, in my book, *La société comme verdict* (Society as a verdict). The record he made in 1971, where he sings his own settings of some of Aragon's poems, is a landmark in France. A number of his songs were huge successes and remain classics. The ones my father loved to sing, "Ma France" (My France) or "Que la montagne est belle" (How beautiful the mountain is), are fine examples of the best work of this politically committed artist. He knew how to draw emotions out of his listeners from the working and popular classes, along with feelings of social and political affiliation; he aimed to give these people visibility as well as dignity in public and in culture. I remember going to hear him when I was a Trotskyist high school student, at the Maison de la culture in Reims, and with a few other persons, I had booed the part of a song in which he compared students on the extreme left with police informants, as was often done by Communist Party officials, whose propaganda he foolishly repeated. We thought of him as a "Stalinist," even though he had denounced the 1968 invasion of Czechoslovakia by the troops of the Warsaw Pact in a 1969 song called "C'est un joli nom, camarade" (Comrade, it's a nice word).[11] When my father ceased being a worker and became a supervisor and then a foreman, which represented for him not simply a promotion, but more importantly a shift in social position, a new "place" within his world, he never gave up liking and singing those Ferrat songs. Others might have been quick to do so, caught up in the desire to establish in that way—especially in their own eyes—some distance between their new and old selves. For my father, it was doubtless a way to stay connected to what he had been for such a long time, to let those people in front of whom he would sing these songs on any festive occasion know that he still felt the same emotions he had always felt, and to go on experiencing, even if intermittently, the class affiliation of which he had been so proud long ago, or rather not so long ago. He was proud no longer to be a worker, but did not forget that he had been one, and that, in a certain way, he still was one.

Jean Ferrat sang about the France of the working class, of those who were exploited, the oppressed, the France of:

five-year-old children working the mines,
the France who built your factories with their own hands,
the France about whom Monsieur Thiers said: "Shoot them
down!"

He extolled the greatness of this France of the people, a France that was forever in revolt, "la belle et la rebelle" (beautiful and rebellious), the France of the Paris Commune of 1871, of the huge strikes of 1936 and May 1968:

The France with thirty-six to sixty-eight candles.[12]

But here, today, I have to mention in connection with my mother another of this singer's songs, "Tu verras, tu seras bien":

We have to be reasonable
You can't go on living like this
Alone if you fell sick
We would be so worried
You'll see you'll be happy there
We'll sort through your affairs
Find the photos you love
[…]
It's strange that a whole life
Can be held in one hand
With the other residents
You'll find lots to talk about
[…]
There's a TV in your room
A pretty garden downstairs

With roses that bloom
In December as in June
You'll see, you'll be happy there[13]

These are, more or less, the same words I said when it was my turn. It was as if I was reciting a text I had learned, the lines of a liturgy that so many others had chanted before me and that so many others would repeat after me: a prayer book for sons and daughters who need to act appropriately faced with a parent whose life will be entirely changed from this decisive moment on. As soon as you open any book where old age is the topic, you rediscover these same sentences, these same conversations.

In the novel *The Way to the Cats*, by Yehoshua Kenaz, one of the characters is hospitalized, and her daughter tries to convince her that she needs to move to a nursing home. The mother resists as best she can, explaining her worries and fears to her daughter, who replies patiently with a series of stereotypical phrases: "Don't be afraid"; "You'll be in a good place"; "We'll see to it that they take good care of you"; "We'll come to see you every few days."[14]

In saying these things that we know to be mostly lies, and in saying them to someone who also knows, or guesses, or foresees that they are lies, what a severely bad conscience we must be trying to exorcise, or to dampen, at the same time as we are trying to reassure the person to whom we are saying such things in a tone so unusually gentle that the falseness is all the more clear! This is what Barney G. Glaser and Anselm L. Strauss have called a "ritual drama of mutual pretense": each party "acts as if," playing roles that are highly codified. The interaction is shaped by this "mutual pretense," with each party pretending to believe the playacting of the other, pretending not to know the truth.[15]

Indeed, it is possible that this reciprocal playacting is so urgently necessary in such situations that everyone does their best despite everything to believe in the fiction, at least a little bit, to take these illusions for provisional truths. And yet reality is never far off and cannot be completely ignored.

I had seen my mother's health decline, her mobility become more and more limited, year after year, and then month after month. The difficulties she had moving about went on increasing to the point where it was nearly impossible for her to do so.

She could herself see this diminishment, and she surely knew, deep inside, that it was irreversible: it wasn't something that she was going to get under control, or something that might improve at all. And yet she went on repeating, "When I'm feeling better…," or "when I'm well again…," as if she could somehow ward off her inability to change the biological course of things, something she had difficulty resigning herself to, but also something, given the state of her health, that could not be resisted. At those moments, I'd reply, "Yes, once you are better…" or "once you are well again…," knowing full well the falseness of my words. But how could anyone say to their mother: "No, you are never going to get better, you'll never be well again…"?

And at the moment she was admitted to the nursing home, how could I have said to her: "I know things will never be the same for you"; "I know you are not going to be happy here in this room"? And when she would say to me, in the days ahead, "When I'll be well enough to leave here," by which she meant move out of the home, and when she would want to find out if a new apartment might open up in Tinqueux, or perhaps even in Muizon, or to find out if I'd agree to her coming to Paris for a few days so she could see the Eiffel Tower again in the magical moment when at nightfall it lights up and sparkles… how could I have said to her that obviously none of that was ever going to happen? How could I tell her that her condition was only going to get worse? How could I reply that she was never going to go back to live in Tinqueux or in Muizon, that she'd never be returning to Paris, never see the Eiffel Tower again, never leave this place, or at least not until…?

It might seem totally obvious, and yet it is necessary to insist on the fact that being admitted to a nursing home marks, in almost every case, a radical point of rupture in someone's life.[16]

It's not some ordinary move, a change of locale, of house, of surroundings. It is an uprooting from your past and your present, a total disruption that causes an emotional shock that it is difficult to evade, and from which it is difficult to recover. All the more so given that everyone who enters into a nursing home knows—and can't help but know despite all the ritual denials and the games of mutual pretense that are played—that it will be their final place of residence.

One doesn't move into a nursing home for a short visit, for a stay more or less long, waiting for the moment when you can return home, return to where you really live. No! It's a permanent move. You will die there. It's not clear when it will happen, but it's clear where. Vladimir Jankélévitch liked to cite a saying in Latin: *mors certa, hora incerta.* "Death is certain, but the time of death is not." What can be added to that is that, once you've moved into one of these establishments, the place is also certain, *locus certus*, more certain than the time, even if the time can't be far off.

In difficult moments like these, another feeling comes to color the dark mood you find yourself immersed in, another feeling from which you can't free yourself. To a deep sadness, a feeling of terror is added. I found myself recalling the first lines of Beckett's novel *Molloy*—I would never have guessed that I had retained such a precise memory of that page, but, in fact, just because you can't recall something doesn't mean you have forgotten it—even though I hadn't reread it in a long time. Why was it these references to Beckett, along with a strong urge to reread all his books, spontaneously popped into my mind at the time? Had his work struck me so deeply? Or is it that it resonates in a particular way at a moment when you are confronting illness, aging, physical decline, and, in a more basic way, the tragic dimension of the human condition? "I am in my mother's room. It's I who live there now. I don't know how I got there. Perhaps in an ambulance, certainly a vehicle of some kind."[17]

We know we will end up living in the same room, probably in the same home. Or at least, we can't help dreading this, even if we don't know when or how we will get there. I don't know when and I don't know how I will get there. In what kind of a vehicle? And who will bring me, since I have no children? My partner, some younger friends? Nurses or ambulance drivers who have been sent by a doctor? During the moment when you find yourself saying to the person who is there in front of you, "You'll see, you'll be happy there," you tremble to imagine the moment when you'll be in the other role, the role of the person someone else is trying to reassure. You promise yourself that when that day comes, you'd rather hear the truth.

In J. M. Coetzee's *L'abattoir de verre* (The glass abattoir), the son and daughter of a writer are trying to convince the writer to move into a nursing home. She stubbornly refuses. They insist.

It's the only way she will be safe. She has already had one "bad fall" that required a hospitalization; she could fall again "and lie unconscious, or with broken limbs."

Because she resists the son's suggestion, he becomes impatient and wants to tell her the truth that she is asking for, the "real truth," which he knows she knows perfectly well: "The real truth is that you are dying. The real truth is that you have one foot in the grave. The real truth is that already you are helpless in the world, and tomorrow you will be even more helpless, and so forth. … The real truth is that you are in no position to negotiate. The real truth is that you cannot say No."

But he cannot manage to say that to her face. All he can say to her is: "The truth is that you are an old woman in need of care."

When he writes to his wife to tell her about his conversation with his mother and his failure to convince her, he proposes a pact of sincerity to his wife. When they find themselves in the same situation, they are to find the courage to tell each other the truth, not to lie…

> Dear Norma, there will come a day when you and I too will need to be told the truth, the real truth. So can we make a pact? Can we promise that we won't lie to each other, that no matter how hard it may be to say the words, we will say them—the words *It is not going to get better, it is going to get worse, and it is going to go on getting worse until it can get no worse, until it is the very worst?*

This part of Coetzee's book is titled "Lies."[18]

II

1

I spent too little time in the nursing home in Fismes to be able to give an accurate description of it. Still, I remember its general appearance and a few striking details.

In the entryway or outside, just in front of the sliding glass doors, several people were seated in wheelchairs, some of them accompanied by visitors (their sons and daughters, most likely, in their fifties and sixties) who were sitting on chairs or benches or who remained standing next to them. In the hallways there were a few residents walking with the help of a cane, or sometimes with a cane in each hand, sliding their feet slowly along the floor. This recalled to me a scene that had stuck with me from Bohumil Hrabal's novel *Harlequin's Millions*, in which the narrator is moving into a retirement home and sketches a portrait of the residents who already inhabit the world she will be living in: "They walked back and forth, though it wasn't really walking, but a kind of shuffling, as if they were cross-country skiing."[19] In my mother's first days at the home, I saw her make these same kinds of movements: it was exactly as if she had put on a pair of skis, but she only advanced centimeter by centimeter, heavy-footed, tentative, and cautious. It had been much the same in her apartment in Tinqueux, when she would stand up with difficulty in order to go from one room to another. But here the slow motion was even slower, almost frozen into what seemed each day more and more like an inevitable immobility. She kept close to the wall on one side for support and to help her keep her balance, and she helped herself with her cane in the other hand. She hadn't put on her slippers, which were quite lightweight, because having anything in contact with the tops of her feet caused her pain. This earned her a reproach from the doctor. "You can't go about barefoot, you could stub your toes and injure yourself," she told my mother before advising me to go to a pharmacy and buy her or send her some medical slippers that would not provoke allergies or irritate her sensitive skin. (I was slow to do this… too slow. Where was my head? How could I have been so neglectful?) It would take her ten minutes or so to cover twenty meters. When I offered to help her, offered her my arm to hold, she refused quite clearly, separating each syllable of the words: "No, I'll do it my-self! I want to do it all-on-my-own, I'll do it my-self!" And she did make it to the place she had decided to go. Her willpower didn't surprise me—I had always known this about her—and I was glad to see it intact: it meant that she wasn't planning on giving way to discouragement, that she wasn't going to give up that little bit of mobility that she still had. She was convinced: if she had the will to do it, her body would manage. And, as it turned out, her body did find a way to obey her will, or rather, her will found a way to make her body do what it wanted, but it was enormously painful and took a great deal of effort. A few days later she told me that she had gone to a singing class. She had enjoyed herself and hummed a few words of a well-known song that she had sung with the group, "L'eau vive" (Like running water) by Guy Béart (the father of the actress Emmanuelle Béart): "My little girl is like the brook, like the current as it runs..." Then she wanted to go to a gymnastics class, and I wondered to myself what gymnastics could mean for people of her age and physical condition. But the teacher was absent, so she made her way back to her room as slowly as she had gone to the wing of the building where these group activities were supposed to take place. I was pleased to note that she had resolved not to "let herself go," to use the expression all the nurses repeated over and over: "It's so important not to let yourself go."

The activities list was pinned to a bulletin board near the dining room: classes and events of all kinds. She was free to choose. We had gone up to the bulletin board together, and as I looked at the sheets of colored papers filled with timetables, I had recoiled a bit: it seemed as if they were fake activities, offered as "diversions" for the residents (using the word in a Pascalian sense), or, putting it bluntly, meant to distract the residents so that they wouldn't be too bored as they waited to die. It resembled a children's nursery, but for older people who had once again become children, but ones for whom there was no future. Even as I encouraged my mother to participate in as many classes and activities as possible, I felt with an intense emotion the depressing character of this situation. It was certainly nothing like what her life had been "before."

She also signed up for outings that were organized regularly: trips by bus to a historical site or a picturesque spot nearby. She seemed to have made up her mind to adapt herself to this new life. I felt reassured.

Still, from the very first night on she began complaining about the other residents whom she had to eat with in the dining hall at the end of the hallway where her room was located. A woman older than her, or in worse physical or mental shape, would stare at her, probably because she didn't recognize the face of this newcomer, and my mother had snapped at her: "What are you staring at me for? You want me to take a picture for you?" When she described this scene to me the next day, I was taken aback: "You shouldn't be so hostile. Maybe she wants to talk to you. Why don't you try to chat with other people during the meal, to get to know them. Maybe you'd get along with a few of them…" She replied indignantly in a voice that suddenly recovered the lively tone she used to have: "Absolutely not. Why should I talk to any of those old ladies?" Basically, she was loudly announcing a kind of refusal to me: she would not accept being abandoned, being shut in with people she didn't know and now found herself obliged to live with; she would not accept having been cut off from the world that had been hers while she still lived "at home," a world she hadn't even had time to mourn, even if it had slowly been reduced to next to nothing—a small number of acquaintances, of visits—over the past few years, and especially over the past few months. From now on, she would never be at home, whatever efforts her sons (including me) might make to convince her to believe something different; she would have to learn to live alongside people she hadn't chosen to live with, to get to know people she had no desire to be connected to, even if it was only at mealtimes.

Moving into a nursing home means not only entering a world inhabited by people of an advanced age and often weakened and diminished physically and mentally; it also means entering into a world where a certain sociability is forced on you, and nearly impossible to avoid. You are uprooted from the world you know, the surroundings that have made up your daily life and that, despite all the changes from age and illness that have shrunk their perimeter and the range of constitutive elements, nonetheless have provided you with the sense of a certain kind of continuity, perhaps even of permanence.

Of course, when we are in grade school or high school or in the workplace (a factory, or an office…), or in our daily life in our neighborhoods, each of us has to spend some of our day immersed in different worlds of obligatory cohabitation, involving people we didn't choose to be with. But within these imposed frameworks of sociability, each of us is more or less free to create preferred relations according to our elective affinities. These choices or preferences arise from likes and dislikes that are shared across different domains, from political or religious or union-based affiliations, or simply from a personal sense of closeness related to feeling comfortable around someone, enjoying chatting in groups of two or three… There is almost always a time and a place for these various kinds of chosen or preferred relationships among all the others that are not. Is this still true in a nursing home? It must sometimes happen, of course. But there was no way not to notice, in my mother's case, the vehemence with which she rose up against the simple evocation of the possibility that she might form ties with other residents of the home.

She complained about being lonely when she lived in her apartment in Tinqueux. Sometimes she would cry, on the phone or when I was visiting: "I'm all alone; it's no fun being by yourself all the time." Yet she was not far from missing her solitude now that she found herself obliged to spend time around women and men with whom she had no desire to "rub elbows," to borrow the phrase she often used to use to refer to informal relationships that grew up between neighbors or coworkers, and that were neither based in necessity nor in friendship, but were rather a kind of informal and unsystematic interaction, chance meetings at the supermarket or in the entryway to the building, an expression that she always used in a pejorative way, in fact, asserting firmly that she didn't like that kind of thing ("I don't like rubbing elbows with ..."), or making a point of denigrating anyone, particularly any woman, who was given to that kind of thing ("That lady is always rubbing elbows with everyone...").

In industrialized societies, Norbert Elias emphasizes, individuals, "as they grow older and weaker, are isolated more and more from society and so from the circle of their family and acquaintances. There is an increasing number of institutions in which only old people, who did not know each other in their earlier years, live together. Even with the prevalent high degree of individualization, most people in our society have before retirement formed affective ties not only within their families but with a larger or smaller circle of friends and acquaintances. Ageing itself usually brings with it an increasing withering of such ties outside the narrowest family circle."

He continues: "Except in the case of old married couples, admission to an old people's home usually means not only the final severing of old affective ties, but also means living together with people with whom the individual has had no positive affective relationships. Physical care by doctors and nursing personnel may be excellent. But at the same time the separation of the old people from normal life, and their congregation with strangers, means loneliness for the individual. I am here concerned not only with sexual needs, which may be quite active into extreme old age, particularly among men, but also with the emotional valencies between people who enjoy being together, who have a certain attachment to each other. Relationships of this kind, too, usually diminish with the transfer to an old people's home and seldom find a replacement there."

His conclusion is a dreadful one, but its correctness struck me when I reread his book: "Many old people's homes are therefore deserts of loneliness."[20]

My mother was eighty-seven years old, and now finding herself surrounded by people in their extreme old age, older than her, some of them no longer in possession of all of their faculties of perception and communication, induced in her a strange state of malaise and rebellion that found expression in episodes of aggressivity toward the women around her, the companions of misfortune in this great tragedy of old age, and the feeling of isolation that is one of its consequences (and for which she reproached us, me and my brothers, by means of indirect but nonetheless quite blunt remarks). Surely this was also a way for her to rebel against the inexorable decline whose increasing effects she experienced in her own body; it was a way of refusing to accept the forecast reflected in the mirror provided by the expressionless face of the woman across from her, who stared at her without a word, without a smile. She was not, and had no desire to be like, that "old lady." She didn't want to become the "old lady" who, it must be said, she already was, or nearly.

Bohumil Hrabal describes at length the flood of impressions and emotions that take hold of someone who has just arrived in the new world that is a nursing home, but which they already know, from outside, since almost everyone has already come to visit a relative, recently or long ago, in a similar kind of establishment. The woman who narrates the book is perfectly able-bodied but has decided, all on her own, to come live in a former castle that has been transformed into a care facility for older people, one that looks down on the town where she used to live with her husband. The retirees who inhabit the facility seem to her numb and dazed; she sees them look at her without seeing her because their gaze is turned inward: "they were looking back, to the old times, when they were young, or perhaps they were still grieving bitterly and angrily about some incident they could do nothing more about, something beyond their control, even though the incident had only now reached maturity, while the reasons for whatever had happened were long since past."[21]

Is this a description that could be applied to the woman who sat across from my mother at the table in the dining room, and who stared at her fixedly? Perhaps she did so without seeing her, sunken as deeply as she was in the silent interior contemplation of her own past. Perhaps she was filled with an impotent despair at no longer having any hold over the events of days gone by, no longer being able to shape what comes next and thereby change something's meaning, and at having even less hold over the events of today—henceforth only being able to experience things in an utterly passive way. I asked myself who this woman might be. Who had she been, when she was young, or as an adult? Had she been a "housewife" or had she had a job, and if so, what job—or even jobs in the plural, if she had had several? Had she belonged to a union? Maybe she had worked in the same factory as my mother or another factory in the same industrial area? Maybe they had participated together in the same strikes? Who knows? Had she been politically active? How had she thought about the historical events, small ones and large ones, of the times she had lived through? And who had she loved? What had she liked to do? What was she thinking now that she was cut off from all of that? Indeed, was she thinking at all? Or was it rather the case that she "wasn't all there anymore," as that cruel common expression puts it in describing the dwindling of someone's mental faculties, the loss of their cognitive abilities? I wanted to know: Who had she been? Who was she?

And what about the other people who were there? What past events, what strata of the social world did they incarnate as they were seated there around the tables in the dining room? What common or divergent histories that, in this context, had no chance of rediscovering each other? What subterranean and unperceived links still joined these isolated individualities to each other now that they had been detached from the contexts of their earlier lives, disaffiliated from all their social or professional or political networks? For, despite their current situation, such links still bound them to a collective past, to a common backdrop that perhaps they hadn't entirely left behind and that they perhaps could have evoked had they agreed to speak to each other.

Aleksandr Solzhenitsyn's book *Cancer Ward* provides a close-up view of these kinds of situations where someone enters into a closed world, more or less cut off from outside life, and finds themselves surrounded by other people they don't know with whom they must then spend their days and nights. In this novel, eight characters (all men) are together in a shared room in a special ward of a Tashkent hospital in the early 1950s. They have not freely chosen to be there; they are there by urgent necessity, having all come to undergo surgical or other kinds of treatments because of a health condition. It is illness that brought them there, but each of them brought along with him his past life, his hopes for the future, and also sis fears that there would be no future for him. Chapter by chapter we hear their personal stories, but most important is the way those stories are juxtaposed with each other, or rather, the way they intersect, superpose themselves on each other, become entangled, or collide.

All this happens to such an extent that this shared room and the ward on which it is situated are transformed as we read into a historico-political crossroads where people who have everything and nothing in common encounter each other—for instance the former prisoner who had been exiled to camps in Siberia and the former Communist Party functionary who eagerly and willingly denounced "traitors" to the nation and to Socialism. Lying in their beds, walking the hallways or in the garden, they are all living in a situation of social equality (or nearly so), to the extent that all of them are equal (or nearly so) in the face of their illness, their treatments, their doctors.

Page after page, personal narrative after personal narrative, conversation after conversation between one set of patients and then another, or with doctors (mostly women), with nurses (also women), and with the women orderlies, secret after secret that is shared between this person and that, what emerges is a general portrait of Soviet society from the 1930s to the 1950s: the war, Stalinism in all its mad repressiveness, the Gulag, deportations and banishments, broken lives, attempts to reinvent oneself despite all of that...

The exchanges, the animosities between certain people, momentary reconciliations made inevitable by the imposed close quarters, all of these kinds of interactions between individuals point the reader to more general questions. One can't help but notice to what an extent these life stories, recounted by the writer in such minute detail, the interactions that are recorded with such sensitivity, only take on meaning if they are placed within the larger group portrait, which itself is only meaningful when seen within the framework of the historical context of the world at large. Individuals who do not know each other still belong to the same political configuration: the person who did the denouncing and the person who was denounced and deported, but also another two characters, a patient and a woman orderly who recognize each other, without having spoken, as former prisoners in the camps, having therefore survived the same terrible ordeals and who in the end find an evening to spend together where the others can't see them, and describe for each other the violence they both had to live through, as did millions of others, without ever understanding what was being held against them. All this happens to such an extent that, at the end of it all, no single individual fate, no personal trajectory, can be thought of separately from all the others because all of them, in fact, are linked up with all the others by the events that shaped all of them together.

While making allowances for obvious differences, it is certainly possible to describe the nursing home in analogous terms—one important difference being that the nursing home residents are not there for a temporary stay. Social, professional, political, cultural, religious, and other differences among the people gathered in this common space seem to be blurred or effaced, and indeed they more or less are, up to a point, because all these disparate past lives now find themselves living together in a common frame, one about which it cannot really be said that it was chosen or, even less, desired. Everyone's circumstances are the same: the same bedrooms, the same beds, the same constraints, the same timetables, the same meals, the same activities, the same staff… It is as if all distinguishing features have been leveled by this generalized uniformity. Yet we might point out that it is not only the differences, but also points of resemblance, forms of collective belonging that have been blurred, pushed into the background, even though the geographical situation of the establishment and what is taken to be its moderate cost might lead one to think that, at least when it comes to social class, its resident population could be characterized as distinctly homogenous. The Fismes EHPAD is not a middle-class nursing home, and the men and women who are admitted and find themselves living there are not part of the middle classes, but rather from the same background as my mother. That she ran into one of my father's former coworkers there and was able to catch up with his wife is a revealing detail.[22]

Aside from these preexisting acquaintanceships—rare even if possible—nothing remained to tie together the people filling these rooms, these hallways, the dining room… It was as if the residents had left their pasts behind them, as if their new living conditions had wiped away not only everything that had in the past made them into recognizable individuals, but also and at the same time all of their forms of collective belonging, everything that had rooted them in the same set of circumstances, in the same class, in the same geographical and political landscape, their shared *habitus.* I can only imagine what it would have been possible to recreate, by tracing back the trajectories of the people seated together around that long table to eat their meals: singularities and commonalities, what individuated them and what they had in common as social determinants (not only a shared sense of class, but also of generation, or gender, or race: white women of an extreme old age from the working class of northeastern France). The individual biographies, the life stories of all these women who seemed to have been forced into a kind of absolute seriality (each of them next to the other, but separated from each other, closed in on themselves), would together make up the portrait of a generation, of a social class, of an era and of the political events, large and small, that had marked it...

The woman narrator in Hrabal's novel continues with her exploration of the retirement home: "And there, under a net, I saw an old woman in white holding the cords between her fingers, she was on her knees peering out the window into the darkness, she looked in my direction, her eyes bulged with terror, her hair hung loose and she had no teeth and when I looked at her again I nearly fell out of the tree, she looked so much like me that I thought she *was* me."[23]

Was this the same kind of feeling that my mother had? Did she think she was seeing her own image in the eyes that were fixed on her? A foreshadowing of what she would soon become? She was being looked at and was trying to escape this gaze. The dramatic force of "the Look," as Sartre so eloquently demonstrated in *Being and Nothingness*, lies in its reciprocity: you are not the only person who holds the power to look at others and in doing so to judge them, to constitute them, to define their being, their identity. They look at you as much as you look at them, and they hold the power to determine your truth however much you might wish to hold the monopoly on the power of determination for yourself as for them.

This is a circle from which you cannot escape—"Hell is other people," says the male character (Garcin) in *No Exit*, a line that has become so famous that one tends to forget its meaning. He says it when he feels the constitutive weight of the gaze of another character (Inez) as it is directed at him. To be looked at (or to feel yourself being looked at) is to be objectified (or to feel yourself objectified). You can't escape from this. Not even in a nursing home. Or especially not there, since it seems, just like the closed space in which people are imprisoned in Sartre's play, to be a perfect example of a space in which this "infernal" situation is achieved. Except, of course, that one is not there for all eternity. "The Other's look," in a nearly pure form, stripped of all masks, of all the subterfuges and flashy disguises found in social life, and reduced to its naked simplicity, is nothing but a brutal reminder: it announces what we are, but also, because nothing much is going to change, it announces what we will be. It is easy to understand why, for Sartre, shame is intrinsically tied to the gaze: the Other sees what we would prefer they not see, or not always be able to see—our body, our face, our gestures, our bearing... Not only does the Other see; they decide what they wish to see, they decide what to remember of what they see. We are taken over by shame. Shame is an ontological structure. In *Insult and the Making of the Gay Self* and in *Une morale du minoritiare* (A minoritarian morality), while I mentioned these indispensable analyses of Sartre's having to do with "the Look," I reinterpreted the affect of shame as more of a "social structure." Shame is an affect caught up in a structure of inferiorization, in a system of power.[24] Any kind of "negative symbolic capital" dooms the person who carries it to the experience of shame, not as a psychological, or individual, or occasional and temporary feeling, nor as an ontological dimension (and therefore a universal one) of human existence, but as the effect, differentially distributed, of belonging to an inferiorized, stigmatized, or stigmatizable category. I could say that I wanted to historicize or sociologize or anthropologize what seemed to me to be too metaphysical in Sartre. Indeed, Sartre himself set out to do this same thing, after having written his great philosophical treatise, *Being and Nothingness*, in *Anti-Semite and Jew*, *Saint Genet*, "Black Orpheus," etc. These are a series of case studies on "the look" as a social and historical structure. This is still my aim. But my mother's urgent plea prompted me to back up a few paces. The feeling of "shame," in the sense of the effect of unease and discomfort produced by the gaze of other people and, even more profoundly, the sense of being imprisoned in your proper being as it is defined by the Other, meets up with the idea of an "ontological structure" as soon as you think of it in relation to the confinement in the time and space of old age and physical decline.

All of that is said with clarity in Hrabal's novel:

> I feel that I'm the only one who really knows what's going on around here. But no, that's not the case at all! I see how the others scrutinize me, I'm constantly surprised at how everyone is always keeping an eye on each other in this place. Everyone is always watching closely to see whether the others aren't looking rather yellowish, or losing weight, every pensioner watches every other pensioner, with no malicious intentions, but only because sooner or later, but inevitably, he sees himself, and only himself, and runs his fingers along his own collapsing face to confirm his suspicions.[25]

New arrivals are, by definition, a little younger, or in any case, a little less weak, than residents who have been there for a while and who present to others an image of what awaits them. My mother's anger must have been based in this: the older woman, or in any case, the woman who was worse off, who sat there in front of her, motionless and without speaking, was further along on the path that my mother was just starting to follow, the path of deterioration and, as Hrabal writes, of a slow death:

> But the people here are more humble than I am, they're modest, they don't flaunt what they know, they may very well know more about this retirement home than I do, but they don't do anything with that knowledge, they have no reason to boast about it, not with words, let alone with their eyes. In that sense these people are further than I am, all I do is disturb them in their quiet and gradual dying.[26]

2

Would my mother adapt to her new life in the nursing home? On the one hand, there was her desire to take part in some of the collective activities, and on the other, her refusal to talk to "all those old ladies" around the tables in the dining room during meals. In which direction would her feelings develop in the days, weeks, and months ahead? Would she succeed in habituating herself (in conforming) to the rules that would be imposed upon her (the strict timetables, for example, over which she would never again have any control), to all of the codes that organized the institution that she had just entered?

Socialization of whatever kind always involves a period of apprenticeship, more or less tacit, more or less explicit and codified, which takes the form of a confrontation with a set of signs and signals, injunctions that are expressed gently or less gently, directives and correctives that come at you from all sides at every moment. Each new experience of socialization or each resocialization necessarily requires the learning of new practices, new behaviors, new ways of being; that is to say, it involves a self-reeducation and a relearning of the relations you have with others within the framework of the new universe into which you are now learning to fit. Learning to live in a nursing home implies a very particular kind of relearning of yourself and your world. What a huge gap separated the daily life my mother had during the time she was working in a factory, for example, and the life that would be hers in the nursing home! When she began working at the Champagne Mechanical Glass Works, she had to learn to be a worker, to respect the hours required of her, the rules and regulations imposed on workers, to carry out the tasks assigned to her, to keep up with the pace of the assembly line in front of which she had to stand for eight hours a day; she had to get to know the other women working there, who had started before her and with whom she would now be spending her days, find her way into their conversations, their habits, their culture. In short, she had to learn to be one of them. Both the factory and the nursing home are institutions governed by constraints and by "discipline," of course, but in one case you have ongoing interactions with dozens of people each day at work. Then, after work, for the women, there is the shopping to be done at the end of the day and the exchange of a few words, two or three, or a simple hello, with the neighbors. In the other case, the possibilities for conversation are much more limited, involving the staff and a few of the other residents, and even the desire to communicate with those people slowly fades and disappears.[27]

In thinking over the way my mother had replied when I suggested that she not shut herself off in a hostile way from her tablemates at dinner, I wondered: Suppose she had moved into an institution three or four years earlier, as we had originally planned, at a time when she had more autonomy and a good deal more energy, would she have acclimated to her new "home" more easily, and would she have tried and even succeeded in building relationships with another person or other people? Would it have interested her to chat with other residents in the afternoon, over a cup of coffee, a cup of tea, or a cup of hot chocolate? Or to watch television in a lounge? Or perhaps to play cards? There was a time when she enjoyed playing belote, a working-class favorite, and I can remember long games where my father was playing against other men in the family, and my mother would sometimes join in when they were short a player or when someone needed to be replaced—men being the authorized players of a game that women could only join in when circumstances allowed. This form of recreation—which could become quite animated—might go on for hours, and it is often the way the evenings ended on Christmas or New Year's. I myself even played on many occasions, when I was fourteen or fifteen, with my father, my older brother, my uncles, my grandfather, my mother.

Yet did this question that had snuck up on me really make any sense? My mother had insisted on staying in her apartment as long as possible, and therefore it seems pointless to ask if it wouldn't have been better for her to move into the nursing home at a moment when it wasn't yet absolutely necessary. Why would she have chosen to do that under those circumstances? Why would she have given up a life whose shape she enjoyed? And, if she had made the decision that would have cut her off from the environment she was used to, wouldn't she have declined just as rapidly as was to be the case a few years later? When in my mind I compare the apartment that she lived in in Tinqueux, reasonably spacious for a single person (a fairly big living room, a bedroom, a kitchen, a bathroom), with the rather cramped room at the nursing home in Fismes, the very idea that she might have chosen to leave one for the other without having to seems ridiculous. She knew that having visitors (for example, her sons or the man she had fallen for) in an EHPAD would be nothing like having visitors in the place she had been living. It would have been more like a hospital visit, as proved to be the case once she was forced to make the move.

The only possibility would therefore have been to find not a room but a one-bedroom suite or a studio, as we had imagined in our earlier plans for her move into some kind of assisted living. But when that possibility presented itself, she refused categorically: it was too far from everything and she didn't want to find herself in the middle of nowhere, cut off from the world, which is to say the city, with its streets and its shops... She would surely have been as unhappy in an institution like that as she ended up being a few years later in the one she ended up in. Clearly living arrangements that would integrate independent studios or apartments for older people within apartment complexes intended for younger renters still involved in active lives, or even mixed in with student accommodations, would help avoid these feelings of uprootedness and exile that new arrivals in retirement homes like the one we found for my mother have to go through. But that is only workable for people who still retain their autonomy or partial autonomy. Otherwise, the serious problems related to the need for medical attention and for assistance in all the tasks of daily life will inevitably come up.

Sometimes children (especially if they are women) will take an older parent in (more often than not the mother). It goes without saying that this is no simple task, and it can easily turn into an unmanageable situation for the children who do so.[28]

As for the people who do not leave their apartments or their houses, for whatever reason, what happens to them once they lose their mobility? An in-home care worker comes by each day to take care of household tasks and help with bathing, and a nurse comes to provide necessary forms of care. These people often live alone, in a kind of permanent solitude, except for the hours when the in-home care worker and the nurse are present—"hours" tightly restricted and carefully monitored by the organizations that employ and supervise these workers—or visits from their relatives or people close to them (never as frequent as they could be and always too short), if there are any left. Quite frequently, on a given day these older people only see the nurse and the care worker, who can only stay for a short while. Longer stays are forbidden and there are other seniors who are waiting for them.[29]

Within the nursing home itself, there is a big difference between, on the one hand, the people who are able to move about on their own, to step outside the home for a few moments, or a few hours, or even a few days, when their family comes to pick them up for a weekend or for a longer period of time during a vacation, or, at least, to go for a walk in the garden… and, on the other hand, those who are "dependent," which is to say that they are no longer capable of leaving their room on their own or even of simply getting up and moving about without help… But this distinction, as significant as it is, shouldn't obscure the fact that in almost every case, moving into a nursing home is linked to a loss of autonomy, be it partial or total.

In any case, my mother rapidly felt isolated, cut off from her earlier life, and more or less denied any kind of social relation or social life. There is a word well suited to describe what she was experiencing: *dereliction.*

As one ages, what Erving Goffman calls the "territories of the self," which is to say the set of rights, of places, of spaces, and of relations that define what we are, are inevitably reduced.[30] The older we get, the more these territories are restricted, in the end becoming nothing more than a *peau de chagrin*.[31] What remains of a "self," what happens to the "self," when next to none of its earlier "territories" remain, and when one has almost no control left over the little, or littler than little, bits that remain?

Old age is a stage of life during which one's connections become reduced to one's family circle. (To grow older is to watch relations with colleagues from work disappear because you are no longer working; similarly with friendships, either because the friends themselves have died one after the other, or because your connection with them has progressively, even inexorably, become more distant until it finally breaks altogether, given the impossibility of getting around to see them.) And by the force of circumstance—geographical separation, professional obligations, vacations abroad... or, quite simply, the routines of daily life, a kind of weariness that sets in, or being short on time—intergenerational family relations only renew themselves during infrequent visits, ones which, even if they are waited for, longed for by those who receive them, are sometimes experienced as a social or moral obligation by those who have to perform them. (Or in any case, these are acts that are performed more out of a duty that has to be carried out than out of a desire to see a relative or a close relation, or out of affection for them.) This is one of the reasons why, during the heat waves that took place in France in the 2000s, the mortality rate among the "elderly" rose so significantly, since there was no one there to look out for them, to make sure they stayed hydrated, for instance, during the time of summer when younger and healthier people had all left on vacation.

3

Life went on in that part of the world (in Reims, in Tinqueux, in Muizon…), of course, but in Fismes, for my shut-in mother, time had stopped, as it did for the narrator of Hrabal's novel, who can observe off in the distance, but still in fact quite close by, the day-to-day business of the town that she had left behind: "I also noticed … that time certainly hadn't stood still in this little town for the people I'd seen streaming back and forth across the square and down the streets and avenues, boarding the buses, that their time was now, that the only time that had stood still was the time when I was happy, nearly all my friends and acquaintances had gone to that great promenade in the sky…"[32]

There are those for whom time goes on, present time, the time of daily activities that unfold throughout the town (moving through the streets, taking the bus, going to work, going shopping…), a time oriented toward the future, short-term or long-term; and then for the narrator it is the opposite, a time that has stopped, because many of those who filled that time, who gave it flesh and substance—friends and relatives—have set out on what my mother also called, using a similar turn of phrase, "the Big Trip." The space around you has been emptied out, the future has been annihilated, which means the present has gone with it, since there can only be a present if it is oriented, by way of a multitude of gestures, towards moments still to come, concrete projects, big ones or small ones, even miniscule ones sometimes, but projects that create personal or familial meanings, or ones tied to friendships, professional or social life, politics... It is not necessary to thematize this organization of time in the way Michel Leiris does when he describes the meticulous manner in which he fills the hours and days to come with scheduled activities, no matter how banal or routine, in order to evade the anxiety that inevitably consumes him when he is confronted with the ontological emptiness of life. Our mind and our body move spontaneously, almost automatically, through time and space in each moment. Our relation to time is inscribed as much in our bodies as it is in our minds, and all of our activities are organized by this coincidence of time with our presence in the world: "I have to get up at seven," "I get off work at six," "I have a doctor's appointment tomorrow," "I'm going to Italy for my vacation," or simply "I'm going to spend this weekend relaxing" or "This weekend I'm going for a walk."

We have our "schedule," our "agenda" (from Latin: "things to be done"), whether formalized in a printed notebook or a digital format (where tasks, dates, places, people to meet are noted down) or improvised from day to day, from hour to hour—or by means of a self-projection into the immediate future or into a more long-term one, something that takes place all on its own in ordinary life and in our daily actions. For after all, my mother, a house cleaner and then a factory worker, obviously never kept an "agenda" in the form of a little notebook whose pages are organized by day or by week, yet she kept everything she had to do in her head. (And here we could speak of a "mental effort" that is required particularly of women.) But once this agenda disappears or loses its usefulness, an initial loss of spatiotemporal reference points is noticeable. This is because at that point one finds oneself cut off from the places and environments in which one moved, including the entire network in which neighbors, shop owners, former colleagues, or even post-office workers, bank tellers, simple passersby, would all cross paths… all the people who formed the web of relations, of conversations, of perceptions to which we were accustomed.

In my mother's case, a second loss of spatiotemporal reference points, an even weightier one, would soon follow this first one and make things much worse: she was increasingly constrained to immobility; the situation worsened day by day and began to wipe out entirely what we might think of as a concrete, practical relation to space and time, which is to say, to the world in its multiple dimensions. She made me think of Winnie from *Happy Days*, more and more deeply buried in the mound that surrounds her and paralyzes her little by little, pulling her down into the depths of the earth. "This will have been another happy day!" Henceforth these would be yesterdays, days from the past, even if such days hadn't always been easy to get through. My mother's bed became the mound in Beckett's play. She was consigned to it, and her life was reduced to reshuffling fragments of memories, rehashing the joys and pains of earlier times alongside the anxieties and pains of today.

My mother's physical health had deteriorated quite quickly, which meant that her slow, interminable perambulations through the facility's hallways had come to an end. Her legs, swollen and misshapen, pained her. For a long time already she had had to wear compression stockings and then bandages wound so tightly that they also hurt her. At the nursing home, she begged the nurses to loosen them a little, but they told her that unfortunately it wasn't possible to do so, since the goal was to prevent phlebitis—*phlebitis*, a terrifying word signifying all kinds of danger. She could no longer get up. She could no longer walk. Inflammation had set in again.

It became serious enough that the facility's doctor decided one night to move her to the hospital in Reims. It took endless patience to find out what was going on at this enormous regional medical center. On the telephone, they transferred me from one service to another and then another, without anyone being able to tell me where she was. I did finally find the service where she was being cared for, and where they had done a series of tests and were waiting for the results. They asked me to call back later.

It was already late in the evening when I called back. The intern informed me: "Her condition isn't serious enough to keep her here. We are sending her back to the nursing home tonight."

"I understand, but could she at least stay until tomorrow morning?"

"No, that's not possible."

I pointed out to him that sending someone of that age and in that condition back to the nursing home, thirty kilometers away, at that hour of the night, didn't seem right. But there was no other solution available because, he added, "I don't have any beds available." I couldn't believe this:

"No beds available, in a hospital in such a large city?"

"No. I'm very sorry."

"She is eighty-seven years old, sick, and exhausted."

"There is nothing else I can do."
"Not even a single night?"
"No."

He assured me more than a dozen times that he regretted the situation, of course, but it just wasn't possible for him to "keep" her for a night. I understood that insisting further would serve no purpose. We weren't even speaking the same language. Mine was one of compassion, of human feelings; he objected to what I said in a cold and administrative tone, based on the sad reality of public hospitals today, for which he was not responsible and about which he could do nothing. As is always the case in these interactions where there are medical professionals on one side and patients and their friends and relatives on the other, what is a painful and difficult moment of life for the latter is, for the doctors, only one case among many that they are dealing with and trying to resolve as part of their daily professional activity. In any case, he could not perform some kind of miracle! He couldn't create beds that didn't exist, since they had been cut significantly by successive governments, on both the right and the left, nor could he add care workers whose numbers we all know have been severely reduced in French hospitals because of the neoliberal policies that have included and continue to include drastic austerity measures. Such is the case in all important areas of public services. The sorry state of public health services in France (and it is not much better in other countries) has been ever so strongly denounced by hospital workers of all kinds, without anything changing. To the contrary, things only continue to get worse. The French government even continued to pursue its lethal policy of reducing hospital beds during the COVID-19 crisis. One might almost be tempted to find it normal to no longer be indignant about the policy. And yet we must continue to be indignant, and to express our indignation loudly and clearly without fail.

So an ambulance took my mother back to Fismes. She got back to her room at 2:00 am. The next day, the doctor at the nursing home did nothing to hide her dissatisfaction. Maybe I should say, rather, her anger.

This round trip between the nursing home in Fismes and the hospital in Reims was the last time my mother was able to leave the facility that was now her residence.

4

My mother's cognitive capacities were declining slowly and surely along with her physical health. The periods of stability, shorter and shorter, were increasingly unable to hide this fact. Aging (or maybe, at this stage, we should say, senescence) produced strange alterations in her relation to reality. Strange, that is, to my eyes; but I imagine such changes are well known by gerontological specialists. As I write this, I am well aware of the euphemisms I am employing. In fact, she "didn't have all her wits about her," or to say it without making recourse to a popular expression, she was delirious, suffering from dementia.

Over the past few months, when she had been awake, at home in the afternoon, still living in her apartment in Tinqueux, she would hear someone singing the "Chant des partisans" (Song of the partisans) in the street outside her windows. She would often tell me this on the telephone. Was she remembering the war years or the years just after? Was this the incarnation of some phantasmatic resurgence of a traumatic past that she could no longer ward off? I later discovered, when I was looking for a document in order to fill out some form or other, that she had the words to this song in one of her cabinet drawers. Why was that? Had one of her favorite singers sung it on television and did she then go and find the lyrics? But where? And how? It is only now that I ask myself all these questions. Once when I was visiting her and we were chatting happily, she suddenly made a gesture to interrupt me and get me to pay attention to something that was happening: she asked me in a worried tone, "Now, listen… Do you hear it, the 'Chant des partisans'" I listened carefully, because, after all, it might have been true… But in fact, I heard nothing. She insisted, "You can't hear it? I swear that I can!" I listened again, I opened the window and looked up and down the street to be sure. There was nothing… That I could not hear anything plunged her into a strange combined state of confusion and despair. She shook her head, repeating, "I really do hear it." Or else there would be dogs sitting on her sofa that would stare at her and talk to her for a long time and then disappear. I think it was during that same visit that she told me that the animals she had described to me several times were there: "There they are, the dogs. You see them next to you, don't you?" To which I responded awkwardly, "No, I don't. There aren't any dogs here." She shook her head, her eyes unfocused, anxious: "Yes, there are… I can see them… Look again…" I stammered, "It's just an illusion," but she repeated, imploringly, "For me, they are real." At night, there would be a man on top of her wardrobe calling to her, "Hey! Hey!" He would wake her up. She would shout at him to leave her alone, but he kept it up. A child outside her window (on the fourth floor) would hold out a piece of cake to her; but no, she didn't want it, she didn't want it… Yet the child refused to go away. All she wanted was to get some sleep, but she was prevented by this odd troop of miscellaneous figures, whose different avatars appeared one after another, disturbing her days and her nights, haunting both her life and her mind. Sometimes the situation was even more serious: a group of armed men appeared at nightfall to massacre the residents of her neighborhood and of the building where she lived. The next day she would still be upset; it was difficult for her to recover from these nighttime terrors.

She was basically living in an alternate reality. It would send her into a state of near despair that I was unable to see or hear anything related to the presence of the animals or the people who inhabited her universe, or rather, these spectral figures that assailed her at all hours. She would cry: "You think I'm crazy, but I'm not. I see them, the dogs, right there, on the sofa..." After a few months had passed, she tried to rationalize the situation: "The nurse explained to me that it's happening in my head: I see and hear these things, but other people can't see or hear them. For me, it's true, but not for anyone else." I agreed, "Yes, that must be it." In fact, that was it, exactly! Then, an hour later, she'd return to the earlier scene: "But they are right there, those dogs, right next to you. You can't see them?"

In Annie Ernaux's *A Woman's Story*, the book she devoted to her mother, Ernaux describes the moment when her mother started to decline: "She started talking to people who weren't there. The first time it happened, I was marking some essays. I put my hands over my ears. I thought, 'It's all over.'"[33] I thought more or less the same thing when my mother began speaking to me about the singer beneath her windows, about the child with the cake, the man on the wardrobe, and the dogs on the sofa. For her too, it was "over." I wondered to myself how quickly the process of physical and mental degradation would take place. My father, who had Alzheimer's, remembered nothing, recognized no one, kept losing everything that was part of his daily life (his glasses). In my mother's case, it was different. She was perfectly lucid; she hadn't lost her memory; she knew who I was when I came to visit; we could chat normally, and what she said was usually coherent… Yet she had hallucinations.

During that period in Tinqueux she always recovered her wits after a few moments of confusion. Even at the nursing home, during the first two or three weeks, her cognitive faculties seemed more or less intact for a large part of each day. She no longer mentioned the apparitions and the voices that had haunted her day and night before she was admitted to the home. It was as if the figures who peopled her life in her apartment had chosen to stay there rather than follow her to Fismes. She was angry about what was happening to her, she complained about everything, but it seemed that she had ceased to have those delusions. She was unhappy, that was clear, but otherwise she seemed to be doing well.

Yet this respite didn't last long. She soon began to be incoherent on the telephone, asking the same question over and over, forgetting that she had already asked it, and I had already answered. She began confusing her four sons: "You know what Didier told me?" "But Maman, I'm Didier here talking to you." "Oh, that's right." And then a few minutes later, "You know what Didier told me?" It went on like that.

During her sleep (she slept as much during the day as at night), and perhaps also due to the heavy doses of medicine she was given, she found herself embarking on long interior voyages from which she would return both exhausted and agitated. Her head would be filled with the scenes from her dreams. She imagined them to be real and would go over and over them until she made up some new ones. There was a certain logic to be found behind all her mental confusion: it had to do, more and more, with the same obsessions—or rather, I should say, with one single obsession. It was linked to something that had been preoccupying her for the past few years. She had latched onto a moment that was over. It continued to exist for her and she didn't want to see it disappear: a passionate love affair (I will describe it in the next chapter), one she continued to pursue in the form of imaginary episodes, preposterous tales as is often the case in dreams, but ones she believed in even when she was no longer asleep. If, according to the Freudian definition, fantasy is a waking dream, there was for her no border between the dreams she had at night and her waking ones. The present for her was therefore not really in the present: it was a chasm into which her mind—pushed by the neurological dysfunction in her brain—fell more and more frequently, a fall that it seemed nothing was now able to prevent. Her present moment no longer belonged to time. Or to real time, in any case. Yet as far as she was concerned it was the present and it was reality.

Was she at least happy, as she went exploring through the strata of what Christa Wolf, in *In the Flesh*, calls an "internal archaeology"?[34] I don't think she was. This too was part and parcel of her affective drama: jealousy, anger, despair... But at least, in this imaginary place, the man she loved was there with her. In real life, he no longer was. He had stopped coming to see her.

In Christa Wolf's book, these dives into the depths of herself end up leading her to relive episodes from her personal history that are inextricably caught up in events, both large and small, from Germany's political history. I wonder if it was the same for my mother when she was asleep, or just dozing, or simply delirious.

"All my temporality has sunk away into timelessness," writes Wolf in this book, in which she is describing her hospitalization after a serious case of peritonitis. "My time is running away from me like non-time."

Caught in this "time warp," it seems impossible to her to look forward to "a time in which the word 'time' will have meaning again … in which there will be a time grid, gain of time and loss of time, time segments, points of time, and time intervals, measures of time and determinations of time, half times and decay times, in which there'll be a before and after, days made up of morning and evening," a time "in which I'll take time or realize that it's high time, choose the right moment in time, or manage to intervene at the wrong time…"[35]

Alas, all she can do is notice that "powerless, indecisive, and without responsibility, I've fallen out of time's net." And that "unsummoned and uncontrollable, clumps of memory drift by the sand bar I'm holding on to in this sea of unconsciousness."[36]

She knows that she is suffering. The pain wipes away her relationship to time and undoes the connection of her body and mind to everything that had created patterns in time, both her time and that of others.

The story she is telling is one of an emergency hospitalization, filled with medical tests (scans), surgery, suffering, fear…

Yet however difficult, however horrible such moments are, the disruption of one's relation to time that they cause—or rather the erasure of time and the fall into a period of "nontime"—remains provisional, as long as the illness is one that can be cured. She will find time again, the feeling of time, the presence of time, I might say, along with her presence in the world.

The transformation of the relation to time of an older person, on the other hand, of someone who is sick and suffering, is a much sharper one, because there is no real hope that the way things used to occur will return, or that it might be possible to rejoin the temporality of time. (This very vocabulary doesn't really work well in the face of longer and longer periods of mental failure that happen more and more frequently. It presupposes that someone is lucid and will remain so.) In these cases, there is no remission possible: there will be no escaping from the time warp in which one has been caught.

My mother would call in the evening; she would call at night. She told me that they had forbidden her to get out of bed, that she was no longer allowed to take showers, that when she rang, no one would come… She added more and more details: she was cold and no one would come close the window, she had soiled herself and no one would come to clean her and change the linens. Her voice sought out in the depths of herself whatever remnants of energy it could find in order to protest, to express her rage… She would leave me long messages, extremely long ones, on my answering machine. I kept a few of them for quite some time, without daring to listen to them over again. Somehow, alas, they got erased. I only realized this when I went to transcribe them. What I remember from them is her panicked and indignant voice.

Was she talking nonsense? Or was she telling the truth when she would launch into those endless recriminations that would leave me on the edge of tears? I wasn't sure whether or not to believe her. Yet the more I learned about EHPADs, the more articles I read that provided excruciating stories and first-hand accounts, the more I was inclined to believe her. What was really going on there? I would call the nurses and the doctor… They told me that it took two aides, two men, to support her when she got out of bed. There weren't enough of them at the facility to allow this to happen every day. It could only happen once a week… The idea that from this point on she could only take a shower once a week, and especially the idea that she could only get out of bed on that same occasion once a week, and that, therefore, she could basically never again leave her room… all this was, obviously, unbearable. If she could no longer get about without help, then obviously what should have happened would be that she would be helped to do so at least once a day: that there would be a wheelchair for her to get to the bathroom, to get out of her room, to get outdoors and get some fresh air in the courtyard, or at least to be seated in her chair for a part of the day. But there weren't enough helpers for any of this.

The bars on either side of her bed were raised up so that she couldn't fall out. The closet where her belongings had been stored was locked, so that she wouldn't be tempted to try despite everything to go get an article of clothing or something else. Everything around her was being fenced off, locked away: bars, locks… space, time. Her tiny bedroom had expanded to become quite large, given that everything that had been available to her, easily to hand, when she first arrived, had now become inaccessible, as if at an enormous distance. Everything was being removed from her, pushed further and further away. It was as if the walls themselves had moved.[37] As for the hallway, the dining room, the rooms where the singing classes or gymnastics took place, it was now as if they existed in a separate, utterly inaccessible universe. When I spoke to her on the telephone, her voice was filled with so much despair that I was overwhelmed. She had no doubt about the fact that hostile forces had conspired to do her harm: "They abuse me here… I don't understand why they abuse me like this… What did I ever do to them?"

What is the right way of understanding what was going on? When she would tell me that they were "abusing" her, it didn't occur to me that she meant they were treating her roughly or being physically violent. Not that one can be certain. It's always possible that a nurse or an aide, faced with endless demands and recriminations from the residents, with their slowness and the awkwardness of their movements, would have given way to some appalling form of behavior as an expression of their impatience, or because they too were being abused by the working conditions imposed upon them, and so would take their revenge on the aged people in their charge. All the articles one reads in newspapers, all the books that are devoted to these questions describe situations like these. When the doctor told me that "your mother fights with the nurses," it hardly surprised me. She felt like a prisoner, and in a certain way, that's what she was. She tried in any way she could, with the feeble resources still available to her, to resist those who in her eyes incarnated the evil forces that kept her locked in. The small amount of energy still available to her was spent in this final form of protest. Perhaps that is what is called the "energy of despair." But I did wonder: How did the nurses or the aides react when my mother resisted them, "fought" with them? It's not a scene I want to represent to myself. I would end up inventing something. The EHPAD in Fismes is a public institution, and I am convinced that one finds in public, as opposed to private, institutions a greater respect for the residents. And yet, even if the staff there was not violent toward her in any way, and never mistreated her—which is what I am inclined to believe—still, the whole situation was a violent one. She was mistreated by the very way that the institution managed her condition, the condition of people like her. Here the word "dependent" took on its most horrific meaning.

The truth is quite simple. In these kinds of institutions, understaffing is the norm, and the aides are forced to run from one room to another to care for the residents in their charge, because in general they only have a few minutes to spend with each person before they have to dash to another room, and then another, in order to respond to the calls of other residents who need them… They end their days worn out, exhausted. They have back pain or shoulder pain or knee pain that only gets worse because of the ways they have to help the residents get out of bed (when that is possible), then move around, and then get back into bed. The turnover in jobs such as these is considerable. Workers don't last long given the pace and the difficulty of the tasks they have to carry out. So here too it is a question of abuse. There is a profound *immorality* in the whole system. That is the word that needs to be used over and over: *immorality*.[38]

A report published by the Public Defender of Rights in France offered a damning account of the "attacks" on the "fundamental rights of older people who are accommodated in EHPADs." It concludes by making a series of recommendations to put an end to what it describes as unacceptable conditions.[39] A second report following up on the "implementation" of these recommendations emphasizes that nothing, or next to nothing, has changed.[40] Everything my mother complained about is included in the examples of "mistreatment" that are listed in these documents. Not being able to get out of bed at least once a day; not being able to take more than one shower a week; having to wear diapers at all times because otherwise bedridden people would have to be helped to get up and go to the bathroom and get cleaned up several times a day… My aim is not to incriminate this or that facility, or any particular EHPAD, and certainly not some particular person: this is a systemic form of abuse. It is rampant everywhere.

Yes, the truth of the situation is simple and sad: as for publicly financed EHPADs, they are dramatically underfunded, as is the case for public hospitals and all sectors of the public health system (among others). When it comes to private EHPADs, the situation is even worse. They are subject to an extreme demand for profitability: profit is what counts, future gains, dividends paid to shareholders. On the internet, or sometimes in my inbox, I see advertisements that vaunt the profitability of investing in EHPADs, offering impressive rates of return. I have doubtless been "tracked," because I did some internet research on nursing homes. Cynical advisors who talk about this "market" use the term "gray gold." Each time I come across one of these images, I feel sick to my stomach.

So it is that precise and damning reports can follow one after the other; devastating inquiries can follow up on previous devastating inquiries; indignant books can follow one after another. They all report on the same situation. Nothing about it changes.

I have thus observed that public nursing homes and hospitals share one thing: what they can offer to people who are ill, to people who are old, to people who are fragile and vulnerable, to any and every person needing "care" of some kind will be deficient, significantly so, or indeed utterly unacceptable. This is because the economic logic dictating minimal expense in the public sector or maximal profit in the private one is firmly in place across the board.

Each conversation I had with my mother, each message that I found on my answering machine, left me in a state of confused helplessness. I kept asking myself the question: Shouldn't we have found a nursing home that would have been more expensive, but where there would have been more staff and the quality of services provided would have been better because it cost more? I became more and more persuaded that this was the case as the days went by and my sense of guilt increased enormously. Shortly thereafter, however, a book showed me that I was wrong: the exorbitant monthly sums charged in certain private facilities reserved for the bourgeoisie (that could mean as much as five or six times what my mother's facility was charging) did nothing to prevent utterly shameful and scandalous situations from arising in them. In fact, this very book provoked a huge scandal (thankfully!), once more drawing attention to the consequences suffered by older people because of a thirst for profit untouched by any sense of morality, any sense of humanity.[41]

In my mother's case, the nursing home proved from the very first moment to be a version of what Goffman calls a "total institution." Here is how he describes this kind of institution: "a place of residence and work where a large number of like-situated individuals, cut off from the wider society for an appreciable period of time, together lead an enclosed, formally administered round of life."[42]

The specific characteristic of the nursing home, as compared to other institutions (the prison, the psychiatric hospital) lies in the fact that it is not a question of "an appreciable period of time," but rather of a final place of residence (and sometimes for a very short time period, since death quickly arrives to put an end to this "enclosed … round of life").

And this "totalitarian" character (that is the word the French translation of Goffman uses) would become more and more pronounced as the days went by. All of her life was under tight control; everything was decided for her. My mother had lost not only her autonomy, but also her freedom; she was no longer a person. That sums it up precisely: depersonalization goes so far for a person of advanced age that they cease to be a person.[43]

5

In his book on William Marshal, George Dubys tells the story of how William, feeling himself losing his strength after so many years of waging war—we are in 1219, and he claims to be more than eighty years old, though he is surely exaggerating—the man who was considered to be "the greatest knight" in the world, decided (in his case it was a conscious decision) that the time had come to leave the earthly world behind… Surrounded by those close to him—his wife, his knights, his eldest son—he states his final wishes. Then he waits for death.[44]

What happened with my mother was fundamentally no different, although it took place in a notably different time, world, and social position. She had led many battles against adversaries much stronger than her throughout her life, but she had always successfully held out against them. Think of how many challenges of all kinds had she faced and overcome! Yet this time, the battle was lost from the outset.

Two of my brothers and their partners, alerted by the doctor, hurried to spend her last moments with her, but it was already almost too late. They found in her room a few words scribbled on a piece of paper, saying what she wanted by way of a funeral. She didn't leave a will, since there was nothing for her to leave to anyone. She had no capital, no patrimony: no money, no assets, either liquid or in property.

A phrase of Bichat's came back to me, whose clarity and remarkable concision had struck me when I was a student with an interest in medicine and biology and taking courses in the philosophy of science: "Life is that group of functions that resist death." It seemed like a remarkable idea to me, even if somewhat abstract: two adversaries confronting each other with, on one side, death attacking from all directions, and clearly the ultimate victor—it is written into our DNA, we would say today—and, on the other side, life as a force that struggles to fend off the assaults of this implacable enemy, to delay its ultimate victory. Bichat was talking about biological functions, of course. But mental health and psychological energy are also crucial. One has to include a taste for life, a desire to be alive, what Schopenhauer would have called a "will to live," among these essential "functions." This implies a relation, however tenuous, to the future, or, quite simply, to the present. To live, after all, is to have a relationship to temporality and, of course, to spatiality: it means having the ability to project oneself into time and into space. With age, by which I mean old age, extreme old age, this ontological relation to space and time is modified, then annulled or destroyed. The foreclosure of spatiality and the annihilation of temporality cause the very defining conditions of human existence to disappear. But keep this in mind: this very situation is relevant to the existence of a very large number of human beings; in a certain manner, we could go so far as to say that it is relevant almost to the totality of human beings, to the extent that growing old is the only way to avoid dying. The increase in life expectancy, which produces the "aging of the population" that is discussed in political speeches and bureaucratic reports, implies that the number of people who are quite old and increasingly dependent is growing and will continue to grow considerably. Life isn't only that part of it when you are in good health; it is also when you are in bad health, and when your capacities are diminished.

My mother could not bear the diminished life that was now hers. What was the point in continuing—in staying alive—if it meant being a prisoner in a room, alone, bedridden, with no chance of ever getting up again, of walking, of moving about? "Where there's hope, there's life," the saying goes. The absence of hope, which leads to despair, can also lead to death. What little strength she still had seemed to have abandoned her, or rather, she voluntarily gave up what little strength she had left. She chose to let herself die.

The facility's doctor had warned me the day that my mother arrived: "Older people who enter into a nursing home are particularly at risk during the first two months." She added, so that I would be sure to appreciate the seriousness of what she was saying: "The risk is quite significant." It is what is called, I was told, the "syndrome de glissement," a destabilizing state of withdrawal and decline.

I have to admit that I had never really thought about such a process before, but it was easy to see what the doctor was talking about. The shock of being uprooted is so great that many people cannot handle it and die soon after this radical and irreversible change in their existence. Still, however strange it might seem to me today, I did not make the connection between these general remarks and my mother's specific situation. I was convinced my mother would overcome the problems linked to this period of adaptation and would get used to her new environment. But that was at a moment when she could still walk, even if with great difficulty, when she still spoke normally and had no problem carrying on conversations with my brother and me, with her friend Yolande, with the doctor and the nurses. It even seemed, during the early days of her "institutionalization," that she was no longer troubled by the cognitive lapses I described earlier, the ones that cropped up only intermittently when she was at home in Tinqueux, and that I did not see recur while I was helping her settle in at Fismes. She did not seem "at risk" to me, certainly not at "quite significant" risk. I was unprepared for the pace at which her mental, physical, and cognitive health would decline. All I could do was admit the degree to which what the doctor had told me was true and fully applicable to my mother: no more than two or three weeks had passed and she was no longer the same person. My reactions were always out of sync with, or, to be more precise, far behind, what was taking place.[45]

A month and a half after our first conversation and her initial warning, which I then came to understand had been specifically addressed to me, the doctor telephoned me to say: "Your mother is refusing to eat or to drink; she won't talk... She is still conscious, though. We communicate by way of her eyes." Shortly after that, she told me: "I am going to transfer her to palliative care tomorrow... You can expect that she will die sometime in the coming week."

I was stunned. Everything was happening so quickly. I had not noticed, or had not wanted to notice, what was happening. Or, more accurately, I had not wanted to admit the true meaning of what I was noticing when I would be speaking to my mother on the telephone and she would once again start to lapse, more and more frequently, into incoherence, or when I would speak to the doctor or the nurses who would describe the situation, and the way it was evolving, to me: she was in decline, and it was only going to get worse. There was no cure.

Sometime in the next week, the doctor had told me.

This was probably just a way of preparing us for the final call. It was all over the next day.

So as it turned out, I never saw my mother again after those two days that I described earlier, when I went to Fismes to help her move into her new "home." As I left to catch the bus after the second afternoon I spent with her, I said, "I'll be back to see you again soon," with no idea that this was the last time I would see her. The thought didn't even cross my mind. I would only know later that this had been the last time! It's always later that one knows. I wish I could remember every detail of this "last time" that I didn't know was that (and had I known it, I would have arranged things so that it wouldn't have been the last time: I would have made sure to come back and see her as soon as possible). When I got back from my vacation in Italy, I had canceled a train ticket to Paris-Reims that I had reserved in order to visit her. I had gotten very sick. I wasn't sure what I had, and I was worried it was a viral infection that I didn't want to pass to her. I went to visit my doctor several times, which led to a series of tests of different kinds, then some imaging and even a night spent in the emergency room at the Cochin Hospital, when things got suddenly worse. My health slowly began to improve; I was starting to move about again… But a trip to Fismes felt like an exhausting expedition! Above all, it didn't seem wise to go to see my mother while I was still sick. I was furious with myself: Why hadn't I insisted at greater length that she come settle in Paris? I was supposed to go deliver a series of lectures in Germany that I had agreed to a long while ago. Even though I was still feeling quite weak, I wanted to keep my promises, thinking that I would go to Reims and Fismes as soon as I got home, three or four days later: I would be feeling better and would finally be able to spend some time with her. It was at this point that I received the series of horrible messages. I hold it against myself, obviously, to have been so slow on the uptake, to have "taken a later train" [*avoir un train de retard*] as the French saying goes. In this case, it turned out to be more than a metaphor.

I try to see her in my mind the way she was the last day I saw her: How was she dressed, what expressions crossed her face, what words did she say as I left?

All those questions I had asked myself thus became meaningless. How many months or years would she be spending in this facility, which is to say in that hallway, in that room. For how many months or years would I be coming to visit her in this large village thirty kilometers outside Reims? She was, in the end, only there seven weeks before she died, and I never returned.

It was only after the fact that I read up on the "syndrome de glissement," because this really was an example of it. It is, according to the French geriatricians who developed the notion, characterized by someone "ceasing to struggle and to deploy all the energy necessary for survival."[46] In the articles devoted to this syndrome, I read that it happens after a physical or psychological shock linked to an illness, a surgical operation, an accident, a death… I also read that "admission into a nursing home when experienced as an abandonment" ranks high on the list of the "shocks" likely to trigger the syndrome.

Some doctors have described it as an "unconscious suicide." But I wonder whether the word "unconscious" is appropriate in such a situation. I described earlier a character in Yehoshua Kenaz's novel *The Way to the Cats* who refused to move into a nursing home, and whose daughter kept repeating that she would be happy there. A little bit later in the novel, we learn that she died there quite quickly:

> She died yesterday! In the institution! She stopped eating! They took her to the hospital! They fed her by force, with a tube! They sent her back to the institution! And she wouldn't touch her food again! They couldn't make her! She wouldn't get out of bed! She didn't want to live…[47]

These aren't individual cases. It's a syndrome. And it is not unconscious: today I am convinced that in my mother's case it was conscious and deliberate, at least partially so. She was certainly in an altered and confused state of consciousness, but one in which she retained sufficient lucidity and willpower to make such a decision and to hold to it. She also "didn't want to live." This required, I am sure, a great deal of courage and determination, and I wonder what was going through her mind in her moments of lucidity, between two periods of delusional dementia, as she made the decision and then waited to die.

Six or seven years earlier, she had had a very serious operation. She was hospitalized repeatedly throughout the last ten years of her life, involving more or less lengthy stays, but this one was particularly long, painful, and dangerous. Her regular doctor, in Muizon, had had her admitted urgently to a private clinic where he knew an excellent surgeon with whom he had gone to school. My mother spent several weeks there, including two weeks in intensive care. She was in a good deal of pain and didn't feel she had the strength to go on. She wasn't far from letting go, from starting to "slide" away. If she managed somewhere deep inside of herself to find the energy that she needed to survive this difficult moment, it is because she was in love.

Three or four years after my father died, she met a man who lived in a village near Muizon. I'm no longer very clear on how they met. Maybe at the supermarket, where he had helped her carry her groceries to the car and put them in the trunk? In any case, they started seeing each other. He would come and spend afternoons with her. She fell in love with him. One time when I had invited her to come spend a few days in Paris, she spoke to me about him on the very first night of her visit. I had gone to meet her at the train station, and we took the bus to the apartment of a friend who was away and where I had arranged for her to stay. We had barely set foot in the apartment when she said to me in a solemn and serious tone:

"I have a question for you."

"I'm all ears!"

"You're a philosopher, so you must know. Is it possible to be in love at my age?"

"But of course, it's possible to be in love at any age. Why do you ask?"

"No reason. I was just curious."

"Are you in love?"

She hesitated for a moment and then said:

"You're going to think I'm crazy…"

"Oh, so you are…"
"Well… yes…"
"With whom?"

She gave me some details about the object of her passion. His name was André. He lived a few kilometers from Muizon. The only problem was that he was married.

She asked me some questions (more for formality's sake, probably):

"What do you think I should do?"

"It's not really my business. You should do what you want to. The important thing is that you should be happy."

"Yes, he makes me happy. Your father never did. But with him I feel good."

"Well, that's great then."

"Yes, I think I'll keep on seeing him. But at my age, I must be a little bit crazy!" (Then she giggled a bit.)

She added that she didn't want to talk about this with my brothers, since she was sure they wouldn't be happy about the news.

But in fact, she couldn't stop herself from talking to them about it a little bit later. And she was right: they were extremely unhappy with the news.

In the following days, I took my mother to see the hall with the dinosaurs at the Jardin des Plantes, and to the Eiffel Tower one evening, from which she came back thrilled. She spoke to me a lot about André.

Only a few weeks had gone by since she had confided in me, when she started to feel quite ill. (Already at the time of her visit she was not doing too well.) Her doctor called an ambulance. She needed to be operated on immediately.

As she left for the clinic, she called each of us to tell us what was going on. She also told us that she had left her keys with the man she was in love with. My brothers were very concerned:

"Maman shouldn't have left her keys with him. We don't know if he can be trusted."

"They're her keys! And she trusts him," I said.

"But we don't know who this guy is. What if he steals something from the house?"

"What is there for him to steal? There's nothing worth stealing…"

"What about Papa's tools in the garage?"

It's true my father was quite a handyman and had a lot of tools… But he'd been dead for several years, and all of his gear, all of his equipment, which filled a good number of cabinets, shelves, and drawers in the garage, was lying around unused, useless. Why were my brothers worried about it?

"No one has used any of that since he died," I objected.

And, to bring this part of the discussion to a close, I ended up adding: "One fourth of all of it belongs to me. He can have my share if he needs it."

(What would I have done with it? When my mother died, it was one of my brothers who took all of it… which was fine by me.)

Then the conversation turned to the relationship itself:

"She's gone crazy," one of my brothers said.

Conversations and phone calls proliferated, and always took the same tone:

"She's taken up with another man, when Papa's only been dead three years."

"But she's eighty years old. Do you think she should have to wait until she turns ninety to meet someone?"

"He's younger than she is…"

To which I objected that, given her age, it was better that way than if he were ten years older.

"He's married."

"Oh really. Whose business is that except theirs? What does it matter to you? Why do you think it's any of your business."

I was annoyed, even dismayed, by the conformism of my brothers, by their moral conservatism. I had the impression I had been teleported into a story of Brecht's, "The Unseemly Old Lady," at the moment when, after her husband's death, this woman changes her life, starts going to the cinema and seeing another man without caring about appearances, nor about what people might say, nor about the disapproving gaze of her children. Only one of her sons insists to the others—who are wondering what has happened to her and suggesting she should see a doctor—that she should be left to do as she pleases, since he finds her "pretty sprightly."

Brecht's female character "lived two lives in succession": the first, longer one "as a daughter, wife, and mother"; the second, much shorter (only a few years) as "an unattached person without responsibilities and with modest but sufficient means." That is to say, she had a few "short years of freedom" after "long years of servitude."[48]

I find an image of my mother in this beautiful, short evocation. My mother had been an abandoned child, had been placed as a house servant at the age of fourteen, had been a cleaning lady, a factory worker… She got married at the age of twenty and had lived for fifty-five years with a man she did not love… Now, a few years past eighty, she had found her freedom and was making a point of enjoying every moment of it. How could anyone blame her? How could anyone imagine they had the right to disapprove? In any case, she had no intention of submitting to the judgment of her sons. She would do as she pleased… Was she going "crazy"? So much the better, if this madness was called "love" and she was happy. She talked to me about him for long periods of time; she was literally obsessed with him. I would smile each time she pronounced his name and say to myself this line from Racine: "Dans quels égarements l'amour jeta ma mère!" (Into what excesses love sent my mother!).[49]

As for me, with a long experience, beginning in adolescence, of stigmatization and ostracization based on a sexuality—my own—that ran contrary to normative frameworks, and as someone who had set up my life in such a way that no one could interfere in my choices, I felt a spontaneous solidarity with her choices, or in any case with her desire not to give them up simply because her children viewed them negatively. And was it not because she had guessed what my reaction would be ("Do whatever you want") that she had spoken to me before telling my brothers? She was counting on the immediate approval of the gay son, and it gave her a certain self-confidence. I don't think a negative reaction from me would have changed anything, but I am persuaded that my reaction made it easier for her to act on what she had wanted to do.

These absurd—and pointless, because what they thought made no real difference to her—discussions with my brothers petered out on their own. They had no choice but to accept the situation. Also, they really had no choice but to admit something that was obvious: if she had survived this operation, if she had put up the necessary fight, it was because she was in love.

While she was still in intensive care, just after her surgery, we were not allowed to spend very much time with her, and I was feeling quite pessimistic: she was complaining of the unceasing pain that afflicted her, despite the large doses of painkillers that she was receiving. Half asleep, she would repeat in tears that she'd rather just "end it" for good. She had said the same thing to her surgeon: "I want to die." She responded with a reproach: "No, you don't. I spent hours and hours working to save you, and I don't want it to be all for nothing. You will do me the courtesy of staying alive, please." But all it took was a visit from André for her to take an interest in life again. The truth was if she wanted to go on living, it was to go on loving him.

I went to see her several times in the clinic after the operation and while she was recuperating. It was an episode of acute diverticulitis that had caused the hospitalization: an inflammation of the diverticula—pouches in the intestinal tract—that can bring about peritonitis in cases where the pouch distends and ruptures. She had had to have a section of her intestine removed. The operation had to be performed under urgent circumstances, and in such a case it is not possible, for fear of infection, to rejoin the two ends immediately. The surgery therefore consists in installing a collection bag that the patient keeps for three months before having a second operation to reestablish a continuous tract. This was, for her, a terrible experience. When the collection bag needed to be changed, a repulsive, nearly unbearable odor filled the room. One day when I had come to visit her just after she had been released from intensive care and I was planning on spending the afternoon with her, I wanted to open the window to let in some fresh air, but she immediately asked me to close it. It was the middle of winter, she was weak, and she was cold. I was nauseated by the smell and couldn't stay in the room. I left and came back fifteen minutes later, but the situation was the same. This only served to upset her even more. She kept telling me in an apologetic tone, "It's not my fault… I just got operated on…" My mother was recovering from major surgery, and I was incapable of overcoming my physical reaction. I had to leave, saying that I would return the following week.

Norbert Elias underscores this point: sickness, the decline of a human being, and dying are far from being odorless, and yet "developed societies inculcate in their members a rather high sensitivity to strong smells."[50]

The perspective Elias provides in terms of social history allows us to better understand our own reactions, and it has the added interest of reinserting our personal repulsions into collective structures of subjectivity, and thereby attenuating a little the feelings of guilt or embarrassment that we feel in such situations. Our senses have been constructed in such a way that our "natural" reflexes are triggered by stimuli that a historically and socially shaped sensibility responds to.

André was apparently less "sensitive" than I was to "strong smells." Or he was sufficiently attached to my mother to set them aside. He came to see her and spent time with her.

She returned home to Muizon, where I had ordered by telephone the delivery and installation of a hospital bed in her living room on the ground floor. There, she continued her recovery from her operation and continued seeing André and speaking to me about him every chance she got. Their relationship lasted a long time. When her first cognitive difficulties became apparent, he began to notice that her behavior seemed strange. She would forget about a package of ham left open on the table and neglect to put it back in the refrigerator. There were other examples of the same kind that became less and less insignificant. But, above all, she began to be quite belligerent with him. She would cause a scene if he was late, or because he didn't come by often enough, or for this or that other reason… She no longer lived in Muizon, but in Tinqueux, on the border of Reims, where it was much less easy for him to come see her as he had done before. She was jealous, extremely so, of the time he devoted to others (especially to his son, who had health problems), and she found it less and less bearable that he hadn't left his wife and moved in with her. As far as I could tell, it had never been a question of him doing so, at least not as far as he was concerned. He ended up deciding the situation was no longer one that he could handle. He sent a message to me and my brothers telling us this. And he left the keys to the apartment on the table. (He had a set of keys.) The love affair was over. She never recovered. Being admitted to the nursing home shortly thereafter was the final blow. Would he come see her one day? She waited and she hoped… But of course, and about this there was nothing that I could say to reassure her, even were he to come, it would no longer be the same. Did he come? I don't know the answer to that question. If he did, it was not enough to change the way things were going. She had already turned a corner.

The end of that love affair put an end to her will to survive.

She did not gather her children around her to say goodbye. She had already broken off contact with us a bit earlier: she wouldn't answer when we called her mobile phone; she wouldn't answer when we asked the operator to connect us to the landline in her room. I asked one of the nurses what was going on: "She complains that her sons are harassing her," she explained to me. It's true that because she never picked up, we kept calling, one after the other, without any kind of a plan, and these successive calls, this endless ringing, had come to bother her. It seemed like a kind of assault. She wanted to be left alone; she wanted to sleep.

My very last conversation with her (but here too I didn't know it would be the last) had left me sad and worried. She was obsessed by the object of her passion and by the end of their relationship.

I had already had occasion to notice the depth of this obsession: when Thomas Ostermeier and his team had come, a few months earlier, to film her with me at her apartment, for his theatrical adaptation of *Returning to Reims*, all at once she started talking about André—while the camera was filming—and to say somewhat inappropriate things: "Oh! He can't get up to too much because he had a heart operation… We don't do much more than cuddle."

I stammered: "Maman, what are you talking about…"

"It's a sign of senility," I said to myself, when they were done filming that sequence. "She's talking normally, and then all of a sudden she goes off the rails."

I was stunned.

I had the same reaction on another occasion, when after several attempts I managed to get hold of her on the telephone. She was delusional throughout the conversation, trapped in her bed at the nursing home, locked in her suffering and her despair:

"I don't remember if I told you that I'm expecting a baby?"

"Um, no, you didn't. But I don't really think that's possible at your age."

"Oh, yes… That's what I thought… But in any case, I'm not going to keep it."

"But Maman…"

"It's because I don't want to see André anymore. He didn't tell me he was married."

"What?"

"I saw him yesterday at the fair in Belgium"

"Yesterday? At the fair in Belgium?"

"Yes, at the amusement park. He was with his wife. He hadn't told me he was married."

"Yes he did, Maman, you knew it from the beginning, because you told me about it just after you met him."

"No, he never told me he was married… So I told him it was all over. I said, 'Get lost, I never want to see you again.'"

"OK, so…"

"So that's why I don't want to keep the baby…"

She had survived hospitalizations and successive surgeries because he came to see her and because she loved him. She no longer wished to survive because she still loved him and he no longer came to see her. Of course, this is only one element among many making up this "unconscious suicide" that seems to me to have been quite conscious. Its causes are multiple, and some of the others are surely just as weighty, or even more so, starting with her nearly total loss of physical autonomy and the virtual imprisonment that she complained about so pitifully.

It nonetheless surprises me not to find unhappiness in love listed as one of the factors that can trigger or worsen the "syndrome de glissement." Perhaps cases including it aren't all that frequent or haven't been sufficiently observed in order to be included in medical descriptions. Given that these kinds of facts of life are almost taboo subjects, they are frequently missed by doctors (whether they are geriatrists or psychologists). Still, the feeling of having been "abandoned" and the fatal consequences that follow from it cannot be limited simply to a family circle. In the clinical landscape, the afflictions of an "unseemly old lady," deeply in love and deathly unhappy, should be accorded their rightful place.

6

In my mother's room at the nursing home, they found a piece of paper on which she had written (or perhaps we should say scrawled, because it was difficult for her to write at that stage) what are often called, in the established usage, her "final wishes." Those who receive such directives almost always feel obliged to respect them. This of course raises the question—the answer to which is not as simple as it might seem—of our social and cultural relationship to people who are dead, to the presence of their absence, to their memory, to the moral duty we impose on ourselves with respect to those who are, after all, no longer with us. (It is a different matter when you are talking about a legal obligation, in the case where these "wishes" have been expressed in the form of a legally binding will, for example, but this concerns only a certain set of questions, inheritances in particular.) What catastrophes the family of the deceased Addie Bundren, in Faulkner's *As I Lay Dying*, could have spared themselves, if her husband hadn't stubbornly insisted on fulfilling her wish to be buried in the town where she was born, forty miles from their farm, thereby obliging them, among other ordeals, to cross a flooding river even though the bridges had been washed out, carrying the coffin in their rickety wagon. Anse Bundren can repeat as often as he likes that he has given his word and therefore has no choice; still one cannot help but ask if it makes any sense to honor that promise whatever the cost (if it weren't for the fact that, if he didn't, there would obviously be nothing to write a novel about, which would have been a shame). One of the sons obviously asks himself the same question I am asking, since he sets fire to the barn of the farmers who are lodging them for the night, and where the coffin is being stored so that vultures can't come settle on it. This doesn't succeed in changing the course of things, since one of his brothers saves the coffin from the fire, allowing the family to continue its epic funereal journey, on which further catastrophes await them.[51]

My mother asked to be cremated and that a priest be present to give a blessing. What meaning did this request have for her? Was it a decision she had made at the last moment, when she wasn't quite all there? Or was it something she had been thinking about for a while? For years and years? I couldn't understand it. A priest? A blessing? She was not a believer. She never went to church. She didn't pray. She had never expressed the slightest sentiment that anyone could have associated with an adherence, even a distant one, to some religious faith… From time to time she would use stock expressions like "when I find myself up there," but it is hard for me to see in these anything other than a conventional way of speaking about her death without mentioning "death" directly. It was the equivalent of another phrase she would also use from time to time: "When I go… I mean, when I go for good…"

I had often noticed, across my life, to what an extent religious ceremonies punctuate working-class life (just as much as they do the lives of other milieux—petit bourgeois, bourgeois, aristocratic…): baptisms, first communions, marriages, and funerals are occasions for family reunions and large meals, either meals of celebration or meals of mourning. I was baptized; I learned the catechism at the church near where we lived. Then there was the ceremony for my "first communion": in the group photos taken at the lunch on that day, dug out of the huge cardboard boxes my mother brought with her when she moved into the home in Fismes, you can see me and my older brother in white albs, eleven and thirteen years old, along with our uncles, aunts, and cousins, in front of my paternal grandmother's house. I have a smile on my face and he is wearing a scowl of discontent at having been forced to submit himself to this charade. I do in fact wonder why our parents made us do this. A friend of mine offered a simple answer: sending kids to the catechism class allowed working parents to keep them busy on the day of the week they didn't have school. That's probably true. But I'm also convinced that there was something else at play in this relation to the clergy and the church in circles that proudly displayed their anticlericalism the rest of the time, often in a brutally direct or even vulgar fashion. I took these photos with me and because they disgusted me, I quickly and impulsively tore them up and threw them away—something I regret having done today, since they constituted fine elements of a social archive from a milieu for which archives are rare.

The church, both as a building and as a cultural framework, had always been the place in which these social and familial moments happened—moments which would then be preserved in photographs. Except for funerals, it seems. I found no photographs of my father's funeral—I don't know if any were taken—and none were taken at my mother's. It is surely because it would seem disrespectful to take photographs under such circumstances. For my father, before his cremation in Reims, my mother organized a funeral mass that was celebrated at the church in Muizon, which is where they were living at the time. It seemed strange to me, given that, while he was alive, he never set foot in a church and, no matter what the occasion was, he would wait outside chatting in the church square with the other men who were there until the ceremony was over. They seemed in this to be following a tacit rule, respected by all who were part of the leftist working class. I really think that the only exception he ever made to this rule was for his own marriage. In my mother's case, a mass in church was, in any case, replaced by a blessing pronounced by a priest at the cremation. And really, who was going to take the trouble to organize a funeral mass for her in the church in Tinqueux, which was situated on the square right in front of the recently constructed public housing in which she had lived for the last few years before ending up in the nursing home in Fismes? In any case, her final scribbles made no mention of it, which was just as well as far as everyone else was concerned.

The one of my brothers who organized the "ceremony" (what else could we call this lugubrious moment?) did just as she requested. He wrote me to inform me of the sequence of events, the day, and the time:

> We have respected her wishes and arranged her funeral as she asked: with a religious blessing, a cremation, and then the scattering of the ashes in the memorial garden. The religious ceremony will take place at the crematorium itself; a priest will be there to welcome us.

Someone's relation to religion, or rather, their relation to religious ceremonies in the absence of any relation to religion, cannot be ascribed to some diffuse and unspoken form of belief or of faith. I can affirm, without running any risk of being contradicted, that such things were totally absent from my family. It rather has to do with an adherence to a kind of ritual scansion of ages and of life (including advance planning for funerals), where the church, both as a building and as an institution, represents a place and a marker that confers a kind of solemnity on moments that hold a place outside of ordinary temporality. All this seems to contribute to maintaining a conformity with what is expected, a conformity with the respectable self-image that one wants to project. Being concerned about the image one projects (to oneself and to others), about dignity and respectability, means that one is required to submit to tradition—to social injunctions that have no other meaning for those who follow them than that they are social injunctions to be followed without thinking about it: that's how it is. It's as simple as that.

It was also, of course, always a matter of making an effort—by recourse to a perennial institution with its liturgy and its decorum—to reestablish and to demonstrate a certain cohesion within the family circle despite all the transformations that had occurred and all the distance that had been created across the decades. Such ceremonies were the occasions for reuniting, for meals at which twenty to thirty people would come together to eat for hours, with the meal punctuated by sessions of photo taking (at least at baptisms, first communions, and weddings) that were much less improvisational than they seemed to be, and that attested to the permanence of the family and to its cohesion, but at the same time also served to produce it, or at least to produce the social fiction of it.

When my mother died, there wasn't much family left to reunite or to "produce." My father's sisters (my aunts who are present in the old photographs of the first communion that I just described) had fallen out with her and so did not show up. André didn't either. So only two of my brothers and their partners came to the crematorium (the third, who lives on La Réunion and who had made the long trip to see her less than two months earlier, did not come back). For my part, I simply wrote to my youngest brother, who had organized everything (and had complained about it in this way: "I'm the youngest, but it's me who has to set everything up"), that I was unable to be there, but that I would come visit him in Rochefort before too long to look for a few documents and photographs in the boxes that he had taken with him when he cleaned out my mother's room at the nursing home. Something I never followed up on.

I couldn't see myself being welcomed by a priest, and even less being blessed by one. What was the point in attending? I had not gone to my father's funeral, and I did not go to my mother's either. The scattering of the ashes in the "Memorial Garden" meant there would be no possibility of later visiting the graves of the departed to meditate or to leave flowers. But really, what would have been the point? What meaning is there in leaving flowers on a piece of stone beneath which the skeleton of someone to whom you were close is turning to dust?

Describing the splendor of the funeral of William Marshal, Duby seems to wax nostalgic. He writes:

> And we, who no longer know the meaning of a *sumptuous death*, we who hide death away, who hush it up, who get rid of

> it as fast as we can—an embarrassing business—we for whom a good death must be swift, discreet, solitary, let us take advantage of the fact that the greatness to which the earl has acceded puts him, for our eyes, in an exceptionally brilliant light. Let us follow step by step, in all the details of its unfolding, the ritual of death in the old style, which was not an evasion, a furtive exit, but a slow, orderly approach, a careful prelude, a solemn transfer from one condition to another, to a higher state, a transition as public as the weddings of the period, as majestic as the entrances of kings into fine cities. The death that we have lost and that, it may well be, we miss.[52]

One might imagine the burials of people of the lower classes as less grandiose, but even beyond that, I wonder what this attraction to the glamor of mourning means. I am not one of those who, often taking their inspiration from works published by Philippe Ariès in the 1970s, mourn the loss of elaborate ceremonial funerals, their dramaturgy, the ostentatious performance of grief and sadness.[53] I have always preferred to mourn my friends alone, or in a small group of intimates. The only funeral that I have attended in the past twenty years was that of Pierre Bourdieu. His family had invited me along with around twenty other close friends. The chance to speak with a few friends and share a few memories brought me some comfort in that bleak moment. But I have never gone back to his grave. I don't visit cemeteries.

I prefer the following remarks by Foucault on death as effacement, a statement that differs markedly from lamentations of Ariès:

Death becomes a non-event. Generally speaking, people die under a blanket of drugs, if not in some accident, so that they lose consciousness entirely in a few hours, a few days, or a few weeks: they fade away [*ils s'effacent*]. We live in a world in which the medical and pharmaceutical accompaniment of death deprives it of much of its pain and drama.

I don't go along entirely with everything that is said about the "asepticization" of death, as opposed to something like an integrating, dramatic ritual. The noisy wailing around the coffin was not always exempt from a certain cynicism: the anticipated pleasure of the legacy may well have been mingled with it. I prefer the gentle sadness of disappearance to this sort of ceremonial.

The way in which one dies nowadays seems to me significant of a sensibility, a system of values that is current today. It seems to me that there is something chimerical about wanting to revive, in a great wave of nostalgia, practices that no longer have any meaning.

Let's try rather to give meaning and beauty to death-effacement.[54]

III

1

I had regretted not having tried to speak to my father until it was too late. But really, between him and me, it had always been too late. What was the precise moment, the exact missed occasion, that I should have regretted? The gap that had grown between us had not been caused by some specific rupture; it was rather the fruit of a slow distancing that had begun quite early on before rapidly becoming absolute, with no possibility of going back. A reconciliation had never been in the cards. I cannot really imagine how we could have engaged in any kind of dialogue, or even had a simple conversation. In truth, I had no desire to see him. But I had wanted things to be different with my mother. I went to see her quite regularly once my father had gone into a clinic for people with Alzheimer's, and even more so after he had died. It was as if his presence had been the main obstacle to a "normal" (whatever meaning that word might have in this context) relation with my mother, or at least one that was less fraught.

We spent a lot of time talking on the telephone. I rediscovered, or rebuilt, a relationship with her. There were difficulties along the way. And I am quite aware that all this was insufficient. My gestures of return and reunion were too parsimonious. My visits were too far apart, and also too short. It was as if I viewed my time as being too precious, or already too full, for me to find more moments to offer her than these rare ones I had resigned myself to giving up.

Given all of this, given that I didn't miss her while she was alive, what grounds do I have to assert that I miss her today? And yet for months after her death I experienced a strange impulse: to call her to ask her a question. But there would obviously be no one at the other end of the line to pick up the phone. The answer to the question is a simple one: something had changed in my life, in my personal identity, in my self-definition. I was a son, and yet now I am one no longer. While she was alive, no matter how far apart or how intermittent our interactions were, and when you get right down to it, no matter how little a son I was able to force myself to be throughout my life (I might as well admit it: I had not wanted to continue being a son, it didn't suit me), I still was one; I was one despite everything. And in fact, is it not something I had returned to being over the past few years, given that I took care of her (at least a little), now that she was old and more and more sick. So yes, a son is what I was, and therefore what I had never really stopped being.

But I am one no longer. In the book that Albert Cohen devoted to his mother, mourning her at the time of her death, we find this piercing observation: "Nevermore will I be a son."[55] It is as if a crack had appeared within his personal identity: having been a son and no longer being one. This is also what happened to me: no longer to be, to realize little by little that I was no longer (this time for real, and not just culturally or mentally) a son.

Personal and social identities are obviously linked to the "places" that you occupy in a variety of systems, and to the relations that you maintain with other people in all of these multiple dimensions of the social world. The death of a parent or of someone close to you produces an affective wound, more or less deep, more or less lasting. It also impinges on that part of your personal identity and your self-definition that came from your relationship with that person. Imre Kertész wrote, "The Archimedean point of our identity is manifestly the *Other*. *Their* exisitence is *my* identitarian consciousness. The absence of the other has brought about, not just mourning and the loss of their affection, but also an uncertainty due to the loss of a certain role." Moreover, when we lose a "role" through the loss of someone dear to us, we might have the impression of committing a "betrayal" of the lost person, and we might feel the need to justify ourselves to ourselves: "We find ourselves so to speak in a constant state of self-justification: mourning is the guilty conscience of the survivor."[56]

It takes time to shed a social "role" and the identity that was consubstantial with it. Perhaps such a "role" even haunts us forever.

This "other" whose absence comes to pass one day might have a number of different faces, a number of personal or social physiognomies, given what considerable variety there can be in the kinds of bonds that attach us to different people: family bonds, bonds of love or friendship, professional bonds, geographic ones, ethnic, cultural, or political ones, bonds based on organizations we belong to, athletic teams, religion, and so on. We are not quite the same person depending on whom we are with: a relative, a close friend, a colleague from work, and so on. It follows that the "identitarian consciousness" resulting from the presence of all of these "others" in our life and, to different degrees, even in the deepest reaches of ourselves, is necessarily plural and composite. And, finally, it is the "synthetic unity" (to invoke the concept that Sartre borrowed from Jaspers) of all these fragmentary and heterogeneous "identities" that constitutes the reality of what we are (even if it is most often the case that the social *habitus*, with its evolutions and reconfigurations, stands as one of the determining principles of this synthetic integration, or, on the contrary, of the tensions that persist within the unstable "unity" of the synthesis). Thus each time that an existential rupture happens in relation to one of these "others," each time a relation dies away or disappears, its absence causes us to lose one of our "roles." This has consequences for—it destabilizes and transforms—the "synthesis" that had grounded the "unity" (always provisional) of someone's personal identity. Here the "role" that is lost is that of a son. It needs to be added that it was the "role" of a son whose parents were from the working class, and therefore also lost is what was left to such a person of the links with that class, one he had left behind long ago. Also, in a certain manner and to a certain degree, what disappears is the "identity," or at least that part of one's personal identity that remained attached to this filial "role."

Still, I have to admit that this "role" as a son, even if it would not be right to reduce it to a set of attitudes and behaviors that were simply being acted out insincerely (and even if that had been the case, the role would nonetheless have existed within social and psychic reality, since it prescribed ways of being and speaking, it imposed those codes, rules, and rites that are part of its definition, and it also shaped the complex and contradictory feelings tied up in all these processes), still it didn't really fit with who I was. I always experienced it as exterior to myself. My fundamental "identity" was my engagement in intellectual work, and, in direct connection to that, my life with my friends, by which I mean friendship as a chosen relationality, as a "style" or an "aesthetic of existence" (to borrow certain expressions that Michel Foucault liked to use), and that have always counted more for me than bonds that are related to birth and granted an official status. It is, in fact, an important question why only family or marital bonds are at present able to receive legal recognition. The bonds of friendship should also be able to do so.[57]

I had, then, remained a son despite everything (I called my mother on her birthday, on Christmas, at New Year's), but there was no doubt about the fact that I was not a very good son. And the definitive disappearance of this "role" as son did not bring me or reveal to me any deeper, more authentic "truth" about what I was and what I am (rather more a friend to my friends than a son to my parents), because that particular truth had already established itself in my adolescence and had only been reaffirmed over time. I could say, for example, that my youthful Trotskyist activism was not only a sign of my allegiance to a particular political ideology; it also corresponded to my desire to create a friendship network, a circle of intellectual relations—there were many teachers and students in the group and not many workers—that would provide me access to everything that was missing from my family circumstances (anything that had anything to do with "culture"). By joining a lively activist community at the age of sixteen for a three- or four-year period, I entered into a world where culture—books, cinema, theater, and so on—carried an obvious privileged status. The political excitement of the years following 1968 and the intellectual effervescence that went along with it—a generalized critique—turns out to have served for me, as it served for many others, as a push toward an interest in critical thinking, theory, and literature.

This politico-intellectual affiliation went hand in hand with a socio-familial disaffiliation. From that moment on I undertook to reduce to its minimum the "role" of son. It was done deliberately; I knew what I was doing and had no regrets. The distance from my family, tightly correlated with a distance from my social background of course, would grow as the years went by, and even faster once I moved to Paris. But, and here there is only the appearance of a paradox, the disappearance of this denied filial identity, partially at the death of my father and then completely at the death of my mother, nonetheless provoked in me (here Kertész is absolutely correct) a kind of "guilty conscience." Even if I didn't experience a need to "justify" myself, I did at least experience the quasi certitude that some kind of sociological and theoretical analysis was necessary in order to understand this "role," its social force and, deriving from that, its affective one. For if you always have to be keeping this role at a distance, reaffirming that you do not wish to take it on or to coincide with it in order to be able to live otherwise than under its normative pressure, that is because it ceaselessly calls itself to your attention through the numerous modalities of its insistent, obvious presence.

It seems necessary to me to add that, strangely, sharing this grief with my brothers, which involved sharing certain kinds of information, carrying out various formalities, meant that a bond was reestablished between us for a certain period, even if it mostly existed remotely (by telephone or email); and if this recreated bond has not continued into the present moment, it nonetheless remains the case that I still share with them, if only tacitly, the memory of my deceased mother. Now and then I have the strange impression that, no longer a son, I have become once

again, vaguely, distantly, a brother and that through that means I remain a son despite everything, because being a brother implies that one has remained a son.

Here is something I wish to underscore: it is best not to psychologize Kertész's compelling remarks. The Durkheimian tradition (in its approach to mourning rituals, but the observation has wider applicability) teaches us that feelings, as Marcel Mauss writes, are "not exclusively psychological phenomena, or physiological, but social phenomena, eminently marked with the sign of non-spontaneity, and of the most perfect obligation." Not only the expression and the manifestation of feelings arise out of social, collective obligations, but the feelings themselves, as such, are in no way individual or spontaneous: they are produced by this social, collective constraint.[58]

The "psychological" force of the family bond is above all a social force: it is the result in large measure of the durable inscription into individual minds, starting in earliest childhood, of the structures of the social world. It is also the result of all the injunctions and all the rituals that contribute to the perpetuation, if not of family feeling, then at least of the feeling of belonging to a family, with all the obligations that are tied to it. Try as you will to distance yourself from your family, to wish to step away from it and liberate yourself from its grasp, you will still be brought back to it by a set of constraints that are all the more effective because they take the form of feelings and of ritual obligations. Pierre Bourdieu offers an excellent description of these two movements, centrifugal and centripetal, of the family as a "body" and the family as a "field," which is to say of the family as "fusion" and as "fission."[59]

This also means that one's relation to the family, to familial "roles," is one of the principles of continuity of one's personal identity, a principle that is not easily dissolved by means of a critique of the "biographical illusion." In a famous article, Bourdieu strove to dismantle the idea of the continuity of an individual "biography" and of the "story of a life," because what defines an individual is the field in which they are inscribed, in which they act and interact, at each moment of their trajectory.[60] The stages of a journey are thus marked by discontinuity. This is undeniable. Yet it seems to me that this discontinuity (which one can always choose to emphasize) is also always tempered by the continuity (which may be more or less pronounced, of course, but which is also something one might also choose to emphasize) of the *habitus*, which is to say by everything that sustains the link between what you have been and what you have become: the past continues to play a role (the diplomas one obtained—or didn't; the courses one took—or didn't; the knowledge one acquired—or didn't; the relationships one built up—or didn't; all of that sustains a form of continuity even while changes are underway).

Consequently, just as the dynamic of family "fission" is opposed by that of family "fusion," so the discontinuity of a trajectory (given that social and therefore personal identity is defined by the successive positions someone occupies in the different fields in which they evolve, in all the meanings of that word) is opposed by a number of factors of continuity, beginning with that imposed by the social and emotional permanence of family bonds ("being a son," "being a daughter," and so on), whether it be situated at the level of one's personal self-definition, the emotions that are attached to that, or at the level of juridical and administrative definitions and the obligations that come along with them. To be mentioned among these would be the continuity of the family name and of identity documents, which require us to provide information about our parents each time we renew them. I remember that once after I had lost my papers, in order to ask for new versions to be prepared for me in Paris, I had to obtain a "birth certificate" from the city hall in Reims and a document certifying my civil status on which were printed the name of my father and his profession, "laborer," at the time of my birth, along with my mother's maiden name and her profession, "house cleaner." I was thus brought back to the family and social identity from which I was at that moment quite distant. (I was in the process of obtaining a new passport in order to go teach at Berkeley.) While I was a student, then while working in the various professions I took up, and therefore moving through the different fields in which my "trajectory" took shape, I would regularly be brought back to the continuity of a "biography" and of a "life story" each time someone would ask me: "What do your parents do?" or "Where do they live?" or "Do you have any brothers and sisters?" or "What do they do?" Or, for example, when my maternal grandmother was admitted to a nursing home in the Paris region, and when her children (my mother, her sister, and the wife of their deceased brother) and her grandchildren (including me and my brothers) received a summons to make an obligatory contribution to her room and board—a legal obligation to cover that part of her lodging and medical expenses that was not covered by social security arrangements. It was in the judge's office where we had been summoned to inform us of this step that I saw my mother's sister for the first time in years, and the shock of familial fission and fusion reproduced itself in a violent fashion when, as soon as we left the office, she uttered some racist remarks about the administrative officer (a young Black woman) who had informed us of our required financial contributions. I found myself reinscribed into the family framework by the force of circumstance. (Obviously I was willing to pay the required sum for my grandmother, and even if I hadn't been, I was legally obliged to.) But I have to say that I would much rather have been informed of this by mail so that I would not have had to listen to my aunt's remarks. If, in this circumstance, I was defined, legally and financially, as a member of my family—a summons to the court building and then monthly withdrawals from my bank account—but also affectively (because I was very fond of my grandmother), still everything about the situation was also reminding me of the inverse reasons—social, intellectual, and political—for which I had been so eager no longer to belong to this family. There have been many occasions on which it has not been easy for me to manage this contradiction, or to try to forget it, because it reasserts itself at regular intervals thanks to those juridico-institutional mechanisms that govern our lives independently of our own will.

After my mother died, my three brothers and I had to sign papers drawn up by a notary, even though she had not left a will, in order to be the beneficiaries of her "inheritance." It is an official affidavit, and I had not known that such a procedure was required, given that after my father's death my mother had been shocked and indignant to learn that a portion of the money in their bank accounts was owed to his sons. She had asked us to sign papers that allowed her to be the sole beneficiary of everything they held in common. As she hammered home to us on the telephone, it "really" was hers, since it was what they had earned and saved together. In that case, no other administrative steps were required. But after her death, the "inheritance" that was ours amounted to dividing up in equal parts what she had deposited over the years in her savings accounts and her life insurance. I was the one who took care of the details for the four of us, passing on to my brothers the bits of information they needed in order to fill out and submit the required paperwork. My oldest brother refused to fill out the forms because, given his mistrustful attitude toward bureaucracy, typical of people from the working classes, he couldn't understand why they wanted so much information from him, in particular about his income and his taxes. I had to explain to him—and to convince him—that if he did not send the form back, none of us could receive our part of the inheritance. This meant he too would be deprived of the sum in question, whereas he was the one of us who most needed it. In order to reassure him, and because I also suspected he was not comfortable with the idea that I would know how much he earned—he lives on welfare in Belgium—I gave him the email address of the notary, and suggested he send the necessary information directly. The final amount each of us ended up receiving was not significant. "Inheritances" in the working classes don't usually amount to much, and it even seems strange to use the same word as the one that designates what is transmitted in bourgeois or aristocratic families. Still, carrying out these tasks once again inscribed me in a familial and social past that was therefore also my present.

It is surely the presence of this insurmountable contradiction between continuity and discontinuity that allows for a concrete understanding of the odd twists and turns of a *habitus*, which is a system of collective constraints that have been inscribed in an individual, and that reach into what is most individual about that individual; it also allows one to see how the reality of a rising trajectory and of a split *habitus* unfolds from day to day. Family as an institution and as a feeling thus represents in both the mind and the body of a class renegade a space of relation, of mediation, and of conflict between the class into which one has moved and the class of origin.

2

However loose it may have become, my bond with my mother placed me within a collective history and a mental geography that can be captured in a single word: family. In her book *Old Age*, Simone de Beauvoir calls attention to societies studied by ethnologists where older people are the keepers of the knowledge of family genealogies.[61] Is it not the same in our own society, despite all the differences one might think of, especially those that have to do with writing and with official record keeping? It is certainly so when it comes to genealogies, and, more widely, to that social memory that is most at risk of disappearing alongside genealogies. The task of remembering in this way usually falls to women, partly because they live longer, on average, than men, but also because, in a general way, women are the ones assigned the task of maintaining family relationships and friendships throughout their lives, and so they keep the register up to date, and understand the complexity of these relationships and the changes that take place within them. So it is that in *Patrimony*, Philip Roth can insist about his mother: "it was she around whose quietly efficient presence the family had continued to cohere," and that she was "the repository of our family past, the historian of our childhood and growing up."[62] The point here extends beyond "family" understood in the narrowest sense of the term. I am acutely aware of this now: my mother's death has cut me off from an entire part of myself which, by way of her, remained connected with family members more or less close and even quite distant. When I came across the name "Eribon" somewhere on the internet beside a name I didn't recognize, I could always ask her, "Do you know who this is?" and she would reply: "Yes, that's one of your father's brother X's sons," or "Yes, that's the wife of X, one of the sons of your father's cousin," and so on. Her genealogical knowledge extended across several generations.

But now I will no longer have access to this kind of information. And so I lose a connection, however distant and vague it may have seemed, to an entire universe of "kinship." My mother's clarifications inevitably reintegrated me into that universe, where I would find my bearings without too much difficulty thanks to the map those few names she mentioned laid out for me, reconnecting me to the mental landscape of my childhood and adolescence as she recreated it for me. This doesn't bother me too much: my curiosity on this topic was vague and intermittent, and not particularly consequential. And in any case, it only had to do, most of the time, with the name that had been passed down on my father's side of the family, and only on the male side there, by marriage and filiation (since the branches of the family tree including the children and grandchildren of my father's sisters carry other names, those of their husbands, as does the branch of my mother's brother, and especially those of his daughters, about whom I have no way of knowing anything, because this "tree" has spread out across a multitude of different patronyms).

Sometimes a family connection might be reestablished by means of a name (that of my father or mother) in a way I wouldn't be expecting. Not so long ago, I was in Lyon attending the opening there of the play that the German director Thomas Ostermeier had adapted from *Returning to Reims*, and it had been advertised that I would attend a discussion with the public after the play. While I was there, I was handed a bundle of letters at the theater that people had left for me. I only read them a few weeks later. One was from the daughter of an uncle of my father's, at whose house we would spend a few days during each summer vacation, in Bergerac, in the Dordogne, where he lived. My great-uncle's daughter—my father's cousin—is these days a doctor in Lyon. On the night in question, she was the doctor on call for the theater. (The social trajectory of this branch of the family is quite different from that of my father and his brothers and sisters.) When I opened her letter, I said to myself that I really needed to reply to her, but I let it go for too long, and after a certain amount of time had passed, it made less and less sense to do so…

On my mother's side, the same experience: at around the same time I received an email from a young woman who wrote that she was my mother's brother's great-granddaughter. She had the same name as her great-grandfather, which of course was also my mother's maiden name. It took me a few moments to reconstruct the family tree. My mother would have been able to provide precise details about all the intermediate steps in this kinship relation: her brother (or, to be exact, her half brother), then her brother's son (and therefore my cousin, who appears in childhood photos next to me and my older brother), then one of his sons, whom I have never met, bearing the same name and passing it on to his children, in particular to his daughter, whose name it still is. I'm not quite sure what precise term designates my family relation to this young woman. Is she my second cousin? My first cousin twice removed, perhaps? Things become complicated when you start writing about matters of kinship. To make sure not to get confused, you would have to construct family trees or draw tables or diagrams. We all have a "family" about which we know nothing, of whose existence we are unaware, except in some abstract or, if I might be allowed the expression, some spectral kind of way. After a certain degree, kinship disappears, vanishes—except perhaps in important bourgeois families, or even more so in aristocratic ones, in which people enjoy laying out, maintaining, describing, uncovering, displaying all these branches of the "family." This young student had gone to the theater in another town and seen the same adaptation of *Returning to Reims.* One of the key components of this play is a film that we shot in Reims, using places that figured in my childhood and adolescence, and that is projected onto a screen above the stage. Right at the beginning, my mother, who had been thrilled to take part in this film, holds an old photograph in her hand—one where my cousin is seen between me and my older brother, on a street in Reims—and comments on it: "That one is Patrick, Jackie and Micheline's kid." (She uses here, as she always did, a popular turn of phrase: *le gamin à* rather than *le fils de*, someone's kid rather than someone's son.) My newly discovered cousin—my first cousin twice removed?—had made the connection to this distant relation—me—about whom she had heard people talking ten years earlier, when she was still a little girl: her grandfather, still proud of his working-class roots, was ranting and raving about his cousin—me—who had, as he put it, "betrayed his class" and had just published a book to brag about it. Having attended the play, she immediately went and bought the book in question. Once she had read it, she wrote me a nice note, since she saw right away that nothing in the book matched what her grandfather (who had not himself read it) had said about it. A kinship relationship was reactivated thanks to a photo that appeared in a play in a theater. We met up and have stayed in touch. It is because of my public visibility as an author that we were able to meet in this way. Had that book not existed, had the adaptation not been made, including the film it wove into the play and a photo that was visible within the film, neither of us would have known the slightest thing about the other's existence.

In the two instances I have just described (and there are others), one sees that the persistence of kinship relationships across time is undeniable, since they can reappear like that after so many years have gone by. But their evanescence is just as undeniable, given that it requires such particular (and therefore rare) circumstances for a thing like this to happen.

All this, of course, led me to ask myself what my reaction would be if I were to learn some day that someone with whom I had such a distant (but also nonetheless somewhat close) kinship relation had become an important literary figure, or someone well known in the worlds of cinema or art or science or politics... Would I want to make something of this family connection, even after all the effort I had made to leave behind, to forget, to refuse everything that linked me to my family, so that it would suddenly become my family again? Well, yes, probably! To claim anything else would be to tell a lie.

My mother's death cut me off from my family "genealogy"; did it not also break the final threads that attached me to the social milieu from which I came? It was a milieu that I had wanted to flee, and only later did I try to rediscover it, something I have managed to do only partially, and with a hesitating kind of rhythm. "I shall never hear the sound of her voice again," writes Annie Ernaux at the end of *A Woman's Story*, having just described her mother's death. "It was her voice, together with her words, her hands, and her way of moving and laughing, which linked the woman I am to the child I once was. The last bond between me and the world I come from has been severed."[63] The same is true for me. It could be said that it was mainly by way of my mother that my present was linked to my past, to my childhood, to the years of my adolescence. She was of course present in my memories of these periods, just as I was in hers, memories that she enjoyed sharing, sometimes with irony, sometimes with acrimony, though most frequently in a simple, factual tone, defending her stories and her versions of the facts when I challenged or contradicted her. I didn't always like it when she described the young boy or the teenager I had been—a version of myself I had wanted to put behind me—or when she recalled things I had said that now struck me as naive or embarrassing, or when she described clothes I would wear that, in retrospect, seemed ridiculous, so typical of a working-class boy whose only way of distinguishing himself from the other boys in his milieu was to look "eccentric," as my mother used to say, even though I stilled looked working-class to the other students at the high school, who, for the most part, came from more privileged backgrounds, both economically and culturally. (These weren't the children of the "grande bourgeoisie" of Reims, of course. They sent their children to the private Catholic schools in the city, where they wouldn't run any danger of being exposed to the "propaganda" of "Communist" teachers who were thought to "populate" public schools. They went where they would be given a traditional and conservative education, safeguarded from the turpitudes of the surrounding world, with its leftist ideas and principles of social justice and secularism.)

There was a day when I went to school wearing an orange shirt and a purple tie and was summoned to the principal's office, who then sent me home because I was inappropriately dressed. (What times those were, when you think back on it!) My father grumbled about the way I dressed, which he found ridiculous (there was no equivalent in his world, certainly not at the factory where he worked). My mother, who shared his view, calmed him down by saying, "It's what's in fashion in the schools," which, of course, made no sense. I must have been thirteen or fourteen. This was shortly before I turned into a Trotskyist activist and an aspiring intellectual, which involved a radical change in the way I dressed and acted: long hair, corduroys, turtlenecks, a duffle coat, Clarks sun boots... My parents found this just as difficult to understand, but at least it was less colorful. It also corresponded better with "high school fashion"—and even more so, in fact, with what was fashionable in universities; the students I was spending time with in my political activities all wore the same thing.

The litany of memories was doubtless for my mother the best, and perhaps the only way, for her to maintain an emotional connection with me: "When you were little..."; "When you were fourteen..."; and so on. How these memories must have been going round in her head in silence during the long years I was absent! She was first and foremost trying to rediscover the moments in which we had lived together. We had twenty years of life in common before I left home, but even that history we hadn't experienced, or at least perceived, in the same way. What she had been able to see of my life, from the time I was fourteen or fifteen, remained for the most part exterior to what it was becoming, at least for me; her version of my life was one I moved further away from day by day. She knew about my political activism, which took up large amounts of my time from the age of sixteen on. The least one could say is that she wasn't particularly happy about it: in her eyes it was a distraction from the attention my studies required, and it could only lead to trouble. But she did not know what I was doing in any detail. My father was called in by the principal at the high school, who filled him in and warned him about the consequences that could result—suspension or expulsion from the school, for example, and, almost certainly, a negative evaluation in my file, which would be an issue if I wished to enroll in preparatory classes for the *grandes écoles* after the *baccalaureate*, so I could take the entrance exam for the École normale supérieure. This was a meaningless threat, since neither my father nor I knew what he was talking about. Still, it provoked quite a crisis. Because of some sort of gender divide, my father said only a sentence or two about it to me. My mother took on the task of expressing their shared anger. "We don't pay for you to go to school so you can sing 'The International' in the high school courtyard," she shouted at me that evening, adding numerous curses and threats: "You're going to quit school and get a job." They couldn't understand it: here I was with the good fortune to pursue a secondary education, a chance they had never had, and instead of being serious about my studies I was spending my time on all these other things. It left them altogether indignant.

She didn't understand much about my secondary studies and even less when, afterward, I began university studies in Reims.

She therefore latched onto whatever fragmentary bits and pieces she could glean from what she saw around the house or from the conversations we would have during the day or over meals. She would see on my desk, in my room, thick volumes of Plato (*The Republic*), Aristotle (his *Metaphysics*), or Kant (*The Critique of Pure Reason*), and must have wondered what all these books were about and what the point of reading them could be. But she never asked any questions about them.

As for the evenings and nights I spent in gay-cruising areas starting at the age of seventeen, my mother knew nothing about them… My night life was a secret life, one I hid from everyone to avoid the opprobrium that fell on anyone who was discovered—or unmasked, you could say—with all the insults and cruel jokes that necessarily followed. Everyone struggled to protect themselves from this. Once, during a lively shouting match between a group of Trotskyists and Communists in the halls of the university, one of the latter hurled "You faggot!" at me—it was a typical way of tarnishing someone, particularly a political adversary. A series of violent replies came back from the group I was with: "Stalinist cop!" "Uptight priest!" "Reactionary pig!" "Fascist!" and so on. A few days later, I noticed him out cruising: insulting others was a way of making his friends believe he wasn't gay, even if they would never have suspected that he was. As for me, I stopped hiding my sexuality at the age of nineteen, or at least I was open about it with those close to me (which meant, at that moment, my Trotskyist comrades in the Ligue communiste). It never crossed my mind to come out to my family. I no longer hid who I was, and made no attempt to conceal anything from them, but given that I was seeing them less and less, and soon not at all, I didn't bother going out of my way to tell them about the life I led and would go on leading. I refused to think of homosexuality as an anomaly that needed to be disclosed to the family; I'd let them figure it out for themselves and told myself that if they hadn't worked it out already, too bad for them.

But then from my side of things, what did I really know of my mother's life? Of the work she did, which she seldom mentioned, or of her feelings and desires, about which she said even less? When I was seventeen or eighteen, I spent a month of summer vacation working in the same factory where she had been for a while, a place which would remain the exhausting setting of her days for nearly two decades more. I was able then to witness what working life was like for women in the factories. At the time, I didn't speak to her about my own life and didn't ask her any questions about hers. She showed no inclination to discuss it herself. When she left work, she preferred to leave the world of the factory behind, forgetting it until she had to go back the next day. How little one knows, really, about one's parents. I didn't know much about her life in the present, except for the time she spent at home, and I knew even less about her earlier life, by which I mean the life she led before getting married and having children. (I could say the same thing about my father.)

Given that she knew almost nothing about me and my activities once I had left home and was living far from her, far from them, she always seemed to focus on the period when we still lived together, which is to say my childhood and my adolescence. When we chatted over coffee in her house in Muizon—once I started spending time with her again after my long absence—she insisted on recalling, even though it annoyed me, things I used to say and attitudes I'd had, mostly from when I was twelve or thirteen or fourteen, sometimes younger, which is to say back during the time when we still communicated. Her insistence prevented me from forgetting all those aspects of that distant past; she brought them back to me with the stories she told about me, or rather, about me and her.

There is a poem in which Louis Aragon, who surely had some entirely different reality in mind when he wrote it, compellingly described this "power to blackmail you" that the words one has thought or spoken in the past continue to hold over our present-day selves:

> Inexorably I carry my past about with me
> That which I was is permanently part of my share of things
> It is as if the words I thought or said
> Still hold a power to blackmail me
> Giving them this terrible advantage over me
> That no wave of my hand can chase away.
>
> Inexorablement je porte mon passé
> Ce que je fus demeure à jamais mon partage
> C'est comme si les mots pensés ou prononcés
> Exerçaient toujours un pouvoir de chantage
> Qui leur donne sur moi ce terrible avantage
> Que je ne puisse pas de la main chasser.[64]

There is a way in which my mother embodied that "power to blackmail me" that always insinuates itself into the act of recalling gestures or words from yesterday or the day before. She had a kind of hold on me: here is what you said back then, here is what you were... And when I would reply "But no!" or "What are you talking about?" she would insist, with a malicious or an indignant tone in her voice: "You're not really going to try to deny it, are you?" In reality, she was attempting to go back, and to bring me back, at least in our minds, to a time when we still lived together, to a time before my departure, to a time even before the distance and the disassociation that had preceded my departure.

Except when she was talking about my childhood, everything she would describe had taken place during the period when I began to change, which is to say to no longer resemble the other boys from my social milieu, to no longer resemble my older brother. What she was describing were the outlines and the first steps in the journey of a class renegade. She had no other label for this at the time than words like "eccentric" or "high school fashion." When is it that a trajectory of upward mobility, either scholarly or social, begins? Where is the starting point in the trajectory of a class renegade? And how does the transformation manifest itself? It is a change not only produced but also demanded by the educational system—that is, if you mean to continue in it and to avoid the elimination planned for people like you. But it is also a transformation that you long for and cobble together as best you can—as it is happening to you or as you are making it happen. What are the harbingers of this change—and when and by whom are they perceived? There is a clear connection to be drawn between the boy of thirteen or fourteen, the one who wore an orange shirt and a purple tie, and the one who at sixteen or seventeen was beginning to play the part of a young intellectual, even if a break is also apparent: the second is pursuing by other means the path begun by the first, even while he repudiates and reworks the original, giving him a more clearly defined appearance, one that makes more sense socially because it is built on models that are more real, and so more appealing.

How did my mother experience the distance I put between us? How did she experience my absence in her life (and, at bottom, that empty space that she was trying to fill when she revisited memories that, in her eyes, we were supposed to share)? What is it like for working-class parents to live through the rising social trajectories of their children which, in different manners and to different degrees, but nearly inevitably, establish a distance between the generation that lacked schooling (or had only a little) and the one that underwent (or is undergoing) that schooling? The difference in the amount of time spent within the educational system (a shorter time for the first group, a longer time for the second) constitutes one of the most powerful factors of the discordance, the disagreement, the "conflict," the mutual "misunderstanding" that is set up between parents and their children. Psychoanalytic interpretation has long sought to mask or minimize the social reasons—the sociological ones—but they are nonetheless obvious. It is crucial to set aside this psychologization of social relations—even when it comes to the level of intrafamilial relations and the ways they evolve—in order to resituate them within the class structure.[65]

With my mother gone, the continuity with my past that was maintained through her, even if tacitly, implicitly, is broken, or enormously loosened. Who else can still tell me anecdotes about the child I had been, and the adolescent I was in the process of becoming? Who can trace for me the map of my family, its genealogy, the family tree? This very continuity that she did her utmost to remind me of and to rebuild was often uncomfortable for me. I had frequently found annoying her status as the privileged, if not the sole, witness of the person I had been at the moment when I began no longer to be what, socially speaking, I was. What, then, is the explanation for the nostalgia I began to feel for all of that, for my acute awareness that it was now absent? I had made a point of making that past disappear, erasing my family from my mind as much as I possibly could. And the past came back because of the strength of familial obligations—experienced as family feeling—when I had to take care of my mother. Now the archivist and historian of my youth is no longer there to tell the story.

Mother Homer Is Dead, the title of Hélène Cixous's book about her mother's death, is rich in implications. Once the memorialist of her life, the cartographer of the branches of a family wiped out or dispersed by Nazism (who knew which members of the family were put to death, which succeeded in escaping and in establishing themselves in exile in different countries), once this woman who could reconstruct the historical chronicle and genealogies of the characters who inhabited this story is gone… once this Homer of a mother is gone, and this simultaneously political and personal *Iliad* is interrupted, how is her daughter to imagine her life, her past, her present? What would she be able to write, if it is not to retrace again and again this German genealogy, her family history, that of her mother and also her own?[66]

My own family history is less tragic, of course, yet I could nonetheless borrow the title of Cixous's magnificent book in order to understand what happens in someone's life when their mother dies: Mother Homer is Dead. And I must now speak of her so that she may live again.

3

I will never again have the chance to hear the expressions my mother used so frequently, her intonation, her manner of speaking (loudly), her accent, her regionalisms. I had been so eager to get rid of that accent and those turns of phrase in order to become someone else, someone in whom nothing would remain of his class origins, of the place of cultural and linguistic inferiority from which he came. To change classes, to change social milieux, meant learning to talk all over again, and wiping out the way one used to talk.

This is why recently I was so happy to discover the existence of a dictionary of "ways of speaking of the Champagne region," written by a professor of linguistics at the University of Reims.[67]

I had the feeling that this would be one of those rare references to which I could turn in order to glean some information about my mother, that it would offer me a few documents from a personal file on her that could fill in for the family archives that did not exist. It would offer, in a certain way, a few fragments of a biography. What I would have really liked, of course, was to be able to open a book such as the one Danilo Kiš invents in his story "The Encyclopedia of the Dead (A Whole Life)." Kiš's narrator is invited to visit a library whose shelves are filled with large volumes that have been filled with the biographies of people who must not be famous in order to have been included, and consequently must not figure in any other encyclopedia. These long notices about unknown people are remarkable in that they contain descriptions of all "human relationships, encounters, landscapes" and a "multitude of details that make up a human life." Every gesture, every thought, the songs hummed as a teenager, "nothing is omitted." And any historical or political event that is reported is mentioned "in accordance with how it affects his life." This is because, for the people who assembled this thesaurus, "every human being is sacred." Kiš's narrator dives into her father's life, someone she knew little about. Everything is there, every place, every moment, every event, no matter how large or small. It continues up to the hospital, up to his death... So she copies down "as much information as possible; I wanted some evidence, for my hours of despair, that my father's life had not been in vain, that there were still people on earth who recorded and accorded value to every life, every affliction, every human existence."[68] If only I could find an encyclopedia article like that on my mother! And on my father. On these working-class people whose individual histories are so rarely recounted. I found a few typed pages related to my father: letters he received from the social security agency dealing with accidents he suffered due to repetitive work conditions (several knee injuries that required surgery and reduced his ability to walk), the layoff letter he was sent at the end of the 1960s by the factory where he worked when it was scaling down its production and therefore also downsizing its workforce. ("We have little choice but to add your name to the list of members of our work force who will be released due to the impending production stoppage.") That's about it. But imagine! How many documents of this kind would I need if I wanted to recount his life.

For my mother, the task is even harder: I have nothing.

That is why this dictionary of speech from the Champagne region struck me as a component, a very partial one, but one with a wealth of a certain kind of information, that would allow me to understand a little bit better who my mother had been. I bought it and immediately began to feverishly explore its pages with a good deal of emotion. I would pause over this or that word or expression, its etymology, its pronunciation, its variants… I had the impression I was once again hearing my mother's voice echoing through these pages… that voice that I would never hear again. I know how strange this might sound to my readers, but it was as if her world came alive before my eyes, including her youth, her whole past…

This kind of "recognition" always confers on particular idioms—ones that register as socially inferior on the linguistic market—a kind of charm and beauty which the domination of legitimate language usually deprives them of in a rather violent way. (That legitimate language is the one taught in schools and spoken in Paris, particularly in cultural or bourgeois milieux.)[69] As I leafed through this book, it was like traveling in time and in space (both geographic and social): I rediscovered the world of my childhood and adolescence in the working-class parts of Reims; behind these words, I could hear family conversations. I had in front of me a sort of portable archive that had preserved a living trace of my past—that past to which my mother had, for so long and until quite recently, been my last connection.

I now take pleasure in once again using these terms when I am with my friends, even if I usually have to explain where they come from and what they mean—"as they say in Reims." Because I am not using them in a context where they would be immediately understood, it is as if I put quotation marks around them and thereby keep in place a distance from this regional and lower-class way of speaking even as I am trying to take it up again. All of my friends, as it turns out, have ways of finding certain words surprising, asking for further explanations and perhaps later also starting to use them in our informal conversations, or comparing them with other words or expressions, different but synonymous, from the region they came from (and put aside by them in much the same way as I put the equivalent aside: "Where I came from, we said…"). In such exchanges, we discover how much each class renegade or geographical renegade has had to reject and repress from their earliest socialization—from that crucial element of socialization that is language—in order to become who they are.

That I learned no longer to use this vocabulary from the Champagne region, or, more specifically, from the Marne region, obviously in no way means that it disappeared from my memory. Many of these words, ones that were regularly used in my family circle (by my mother, and even more by my aunts and uncles…), are still there in my mind. For quite some time, these words and expressions, these rhythmic patterns, were there waiting to slip out surreptitiously in the phrases I would pronounce (*bâche* instead of *serpillière* for the rag you mop the floor with; *s'entrucher* instead of *avaler de travers* when something you are eating goes down the wrong way), before the acquired linguistic superego would quickly step in and pull them back to be censured—a vigilant superego that would rarely be caught off guard. How much attention and discipline that self-education took at the beginning!

The author of the dictionary emphasizes in his preface that people often keep up an "affective" relation with this regional form of speech, to the extent that it is tied to family memories. When this linguist would interview people living in the region to find out if they knew this or that word or expression, they would reply "Oh yes, Maman would say that," but then they would add that not only do they still know these words and expressions, but sometimes they also use them, and that usage is more frequent if they still live in the region. For a good number of the words that he includes in his dictionary, I too could have responded, "Oh yes, Maman would say that." But I began quite early on not to use them, to reform the way I spoke, because it was not compatible with the world I encountered at school—at the high school, at the university. The teachers did not speak with the accent of the region, and did not use its lexicon, an accent and lexicon that were current above all in working-class environments, even if their diffusion covered a wider area, socially speaking. Also, anything having to do with writing for school of course served as an implacable mechanism for eliminating any kind of language that did not conform to the norms of "proper French." The same mechanism consequently served to eliminate anyone who could not manage to shape themselves to these norms. For several years, there was a division in me between the French that was predominant in my family and the French that was predominant at school.

After having fled my family, I was all the quicker to cease using (completely!) this way of speaking from Reims—or whatever of it I still used—because it sounded so out of place in the place I found myself—in Paris—and in the circles (cultivated people from the middle ranges of the middle classes) that formed the social world in which I existed. In these circles, "Champagne-region ways of speaking," like any regional forms of speech, will sound strange and will identify anyone from outside of Paris who continues to use them as "provincial" or as being from the "country." You learn this by the way people look at you strangely or by the comic remarks made by those who are sure of the legitimacy and the social superiority of the language that they speak. You discover, to your astonishment, that some word that you have used forever is unknown to those you are currently talking to, and that it offends their ears, accustomed to "proper usage." You quickly understand that such words need to be eliminated from your vocabulary. The language of those who are dominant is the dominant language, the legitimate one. The paradigmatic example of this feeling of linguistic superiority on the part of dominant people might well be the one offered to us by the narrator of *In Search of Lost Time*, in the way he dwells with delight on the mistakes that Françoise, the family servant, makes in her French.[70]

The linguistic situation, the social circumstances of an act of communication, are determinative of any exchange, any interaction. When I would be speaking with my mother and she would use a word or a formula that I had stopped using long ago, I would understand what she was saying, of course, and I would reply to her accordingly. I thereby indicated that the word or the formula belonged to a register that I still controlled. Just because you have stopped using a term, deliberately set it aside—in an act of refusal or rejection—does not mean that the term has become unknown to you. This is just as true, or even truer, in the case of regional languages, dialects, patois (just as it would be for a different language spoken by immigrant parents and abandoned by the next generation): class renegades scarcely speak such languages in the places they now live, but they still more or less understand them, and can take them up again, speaking them more or less well, for a few hours or a few days, during a telephone conversation or a visit to the family in the place of origin.

I will not go so far as to say that my mother and I found ourselves in a bilingual, or quasi-bilingual, situation (the language she spoke was not a foreign one or a patois), but she used words, turns of phrase, and grammatical structures, along with intonations and stress patterns, that were extremely different from my own, and I would find myself switching linguistic registers to come closer to hers. For not only did I know and understand the vocabulary and the expressions she would use, I also knew how to use them, at least in part. It was as if I would return to my mother tongue, to the language of my childhood, when linguistic circumstances demanded it. We spoke the same language (French), without exactly doing so. The distance between our two versions had to do both with geography and with social class. Her "Champagne-region speech" was that of the working classes of the region around Reims; my "Parisian way of speaking" was that of intellectual circles in the capital. It wasn't just that she spoke like people from Reims; it was also that she spoke like a worker. (There is also a rural version of this regional way of speaking.) It wasn't just that I spoke "Parisian"; I also spoke "bourgeois." Her way of speaking was intrinsically tied to her social *habitus* and tightly linked to her body, the stances her body took (as is, of course, the case in all social classes). There is no doubt that she would not have understood, or would have poorly understood, certain words that I use in my normal speech, and had I not made an effort to come back, to some degree, to the language I had abandoned, she would also have been disconcerted by the register I use in my professional life, with my friends, and so on, with its involuted syntax and its complex grammatical structures. It was important to me not to upset or offend her, not to put her in an uncomfortable position in which she would be made to feel inferior. Language carries such violence with it even in its most banal usages. Any slip from this tacit rule by which I adjusted my speech would have earned me (sometimes did earn me) an ironic call to order: "Oh my! The way you talk!" or "There's Mr. Philosopher talking again!" or "Of course, Mr. Professor, of course!" Spontaneously, or nearly so, which is to say without thinking about it too much or consciously deciding anything because it was simply what the interaction called for, and yet also involving a kind of self-control at each moment to censor as much as possible all that came from a bourgeois ideal of correct speaking—I changed my voice, my sentences, my words… of course without being able to modify everything. In short, I spoke to her in a mix of her language and of mine, or to be more precise: a mix of her language, which had also been mine earlier in life and which I still knew, and the language that I actually speak today. Did something similar happen for her? Did she adapt her language when she was with me in order to come closer to what she imagined to be correct usage, which she didn't fully control even if sometimes she would do her utmost to talk the way they talked on television? Perhaps she did. But mostly she spoke the way she always had, the way we used to speak, both of us, in the past, a long time ago. When speaking to me, when we were back together, there was no need for her to change, even if she sometimes felt like she should.

When I was with her, my entire mental and bodily attitude changed, before changing back again once I left her. In the bus or on the train returning to Paris, as I opened a book or spoke to someone on the telephone, I would once again become that social "self" that I had been before I arrived at her place or at the nursing home, a self I had more or less set aside for a few hours.

A split *habitus* also means that once you have changed class, you carry within yourself two linguistic registers, two sets of bodily customs, and that you can pass back and forth between them to a certain extent, without being quite as much at ease in one of them, because your acquired *habitus* has long ago won out over the original one and the more time that passes, the more that latter one tends to become blurred, to be erased. My mother's death will only reinforce, or rather, affirm, this erasure.

When I spoke to my mother, our "levels" of discourse would end up being more or less equivalent. She had her way of speaking and I had mine, which I tried to modify to bring closer to hers. It does not work like this in the social world, where linguistic registers and forms of cultural mastery—or a lack of it—are highly hierarchical. Would anyone think of using popular speech or a form of patois in a written assignment or in an oral examination at school or at university? (It is unlikely to happen and if it did, it would not be a good sign for the candidate.) Would it happen in a civil service interview or an admissions interview for a competitive academic institution or a job interview for some nonmanual kind of position? When you come from a working-class background, in order to succeed in academic or university examinations it is absolutely necessary to leave behind or to put aside the language that you spoke with your family or in your neighborhood (even if you still live there or visit regularly). That is a huge difference compared to those whose original language is the legitimate one.

It would be just as unthinkable in the world of journalism—print or radio or television. We know, for instance, that on television regional accents are almost totally absent because they are explicitly prohibited, banished, except in the case of sports announcers, when a particular kind of sport is attached to a particular region (through its players and thus its commentators), and therefore to a particular accent (Southern French accents for rugby, for example). This is also true for working-class forms of speech, popular speech, popular Parisian accents, the *accent des faubourg* as they used to say, and it is assuredly true for the accent of the *quartiers* and the *banlieues* today, whatever category of the population is being referred to by these designations. In her book *Respectable: The Experience of Class*, Lynsey Hanley describes how, when she wanted to study English literature at Oxford, during her admissions interview one of the tutors asked her to read a Wordsworth sonnet. She made a conscious effort to pronounce each word as she believed it should be pronounced, to give a rhythm to her reading that corresponded to how she heard poems read aloud during her childhood. Alas, her working-class Birmingham accent and elocution meant that she necessarily failed the entrance exam. The tutor stopped her after a few seconds. The scene she describes is a violent one: class violence in its simplest form, clear and brutal. How many failures at school and at university happen in an analogous but perhaps less visible way, because of a failure to master the dominant language?[71]

Albert Cohen writes that "to weep for one's mother is to weep for one's childhood" and for one's "youth that is no more."[72] This seems exactly right. But it is also to recuperate certain forgotten or denied aspects of it, in particular those aspects that one was ashamed of. "I am introducing you to everyone now," he announces about his dead mother, "proud of you, proud of your Oriental accent, proud of your incorrect French, passionately proud of your ignorance of fine ways." Yet he still has to add, "It's a bit late in the day for such pride."[73] He offers the following admonition to us all:

> Sons of mothers who are still alive, never again forget that your mothers are mortal. I shall not have written in vain if one of you, after reading my song of death, is one evening gentler with his mother because of me and my mother … These words addressed to you, sons of mothers who are still alive, are the only condolences I can offer myself. While there is yet time, sons, while she is yet there, make haste … But I know what you are like. Nothing will stir you from your crazy indifference as long as your mothers are alive. No son really knows that his mother will die, and all sons grow angry and impatient with their mothers, madmen that they are, but so swiftly punished.[74]

4

My mother would spend entire days in front of the television; it was on from morning to night with the volume turned up, even when I would come to spend the afternoon with her. The noise would end up exasperating me, at which point I would have to ask: "Could you just turn the TV off?" She would sigh as if I had made some unheard-of demand, pick up the remote, and mute the sound. More often than not, she would continue watching her favorite shows; she couldn't bear missing them.

It had been like this ever since my parents had managed to buy a television in the 1960s: they watched it every night, after dinner (they ate early) and before going to bed (also early). Since my mother's retirement, and even more so once she stopped going out much, it was not just her only way of amusing herself; it was probably the only thing she did. What else could she have done? But it led to difficult moments, as when she would give way to racist commentaries on whatever she was watching. Once on a variety show a former tennis player, now a singer, was a guest and on that afternoon he had invited his friends to join him on the air. My mother: "He didn't have to only invite Black people." Then she would make a point of adding, to the extent that she felt now obliged to accompany her most shockingly racist remarks with a few attenuating qualifications (she started doing this after she read in *Returning to Reims* that I found such remarks difficult to tolerate and that it was one of the reasons we had grown distant): "You know I'm not racist, but he's really going too far." I only came to see her once every two or three months, so I didn't see the point in arguing with her. In any case, it would not have changed anything about her way of seeing the world and of reacting to things. So I only offered a small objection: "But all he did was invite his friends, isn't that the point of the show?" She wasn't having it: "He doesn't just have Black friends." Basically we had here two visions of the world or of a self that found themselves face to face in slightly absurd conversations like this one: I found myself pleased that it wasn't only white people one saw on an entertainment show even if, in this case, the Black people found themselves limited to this one particular show, and invited as a group because they were athletes or singers, invited by a famous friend who was thereby able to make their presence felt at the same time as his. She took offence at what she considered an invasion of her private space (the television in her living room) by people she didn't like, without really knowing why, people she thought shouldn't be there—and, on top of it all, so many of them. One of them by himself would have been OK because as for "him," as she told me at least a dozen times, she liked him just fine. But a bunch of them—his friends—in a group, absolutely not![75]

I had been reading a little before this Henry Louis Gates Jr.'s autobiography, *Colored People*, in which he tells of how, during his childhood in the 1950s, "Lord knows, we weren't going to learn how to be colored by watching television." It was rare to see Black people on the little screen. Indeed it was an event for Black people when one of them did appear on a program or in a series. Whoever was watching and saw them would begin to shout, "Colored, colored, on Channel Two." You would call friends and family on the telephone to let them know, or you would stand on the front porch to tell the neighbors, so that no one would miss such a moment, as precious as it was rare.[76]

For any minority, as we know, finding a public image of themselves—on television, at the movies, in literature, in politics…—even if that image is distorted or devalorizing, takes on a considerable amount of importance. The simple chance to see and identify yourself, or, even more importantly, the possibility to think of yourself as what you are, to learn to become and therefore to shape what you are, is a formative moment in the construction of what is both a personal and a collective identity. For example, when Gates is fifteen years old, he reads James Baldwin's *Notes of a Native Son* with great enthusiasm.[77] We look for ourselves in books, we look to understand our present by linking it to the past, to history, to others like us who preceded us or who are our contemporaries… Any dominated, stigmatized, or minoritized category turns to books and libraries, to available images and representations.

I remember when I was seventeen, or around that age, I saw or heard that there was going to be a radio broadcast about homosexuality. I wasn't able to listen to it, because I was in class at high school at the time it was on the air and in those days there was no internet, so it was not possible to listen to the program later. I hesitated for a long time, but then decided to write to the program's host to ask if they could send me a recording of the broadcast. I did have a tape recorder after all. Someone speaking about homosexuality on the radio was someone speaking about me, really, about what I was, or, more precisely, about what I didn't dare to be but ardently wanted to find a way to become. The very idea of such a broadcast therefore produced a strange feeling of disorientation in me, a mixture of distress and of hope. I received a reply a short time later: they didn't distribute recordings of their broadcasts. I should have expected as much. How could they have sent recordings of them to everyone who wanted one? But back then I was naive and understood little to nothing about these kinds of things. I was hugely disappointed and immensely sad (but at the same time relieved of the fear that my mother would have come across the envelope in the mail and opened it before giving it to me, or asked me what was in it). I was isolated. I was alone, or nearly so, with just a few others whose shapes I would see moving discretely in the evenings or at night in the public parks or other cruising areas whose existence I had recently discovered. In any case, I felt alone, and I was looking for any sign, any trace of something that would allow me to feel that I wasn't alone or that would teach me something about who I was, something about who the people like me were. One day I heard on the evening news broadcast of that same radio station that a demonstration by homosexuals had taken place in Milan—several dozen of them, they said. It left me taken aback: How was it possible to be open about this in public? How was it possible to say what could not or should not be said, what needed to remain a secret if you didn't want to expose yourself to insults and to attacks? How was it possible to find the courage to face up to this opprobrium? I was convinced that, in my own case, it would never be possible. I now know that it is because some people did this when it was so difficult to do that others were able to do so after them—because, thanks to them, it became much less difficult. At that moment, along with my initial astonishment, I felt a certain kind of uncertainty, maybe even a kind of worry: What did this news mean to me? Alongside my permanent fear of being discovered, there was now the fascinating idea that for others it was possible not to remain hidden. These presences within public space that are brought to our attention through various channels act as catalysts: you can see yourself in the new kind of light that they emit, the mirror that they hold up, and the possibilities that they announce. If I had had any gay friends, I could have called them so they wouldn't miss the moment: "Homos on Europe 1! Homos on Europe 1!" At that time, there was no one for me to call to announce any such thing. It would be books that came to my rescue: Jean Genet's novels and the book that Sartre wrote about Genet (which I still think of, so many years after reading it for the first time with such feverish excitement, as one of the books that has been the most important in my life, and one of the greatest books I have ever read).

But when the visibility of those who belong to a stigmatized minority group, one that is subject to discrimination, starts to grow, when it is a minority that up to that point had been kept nearly invisible in the public sphere (in politics, in the media, in culture…), and especially when the representation that occurs no longer involves an assignation to an inferiorized position, no longer conforms to stereotypes, it can provoke hostile reactions in those belonging to the majority, the dominant group, who see their hegemony contested and destabilized. "We are overrun by gays," complained one reactionary French politician in the 1990s, in a set of remarks she made at the time of the debates around legal recognition for same-sex couples. What my mother expressed was basically an analogous sentiment about Black people. She too felt herself "overrun." Her remarks weren't that distant from the exclamations heard in Gates's family ("Colored on Channel Two!"), but they were uttered from the opposing point of view. What she said to me that day, and the tone in which she said it, could be boiled down to an identical exclamation: "Black people on France 2! Black people on France 2!" In her case, however, it was not a form of rejoicing, but rather a complaint and an expression of indignation.

In this instance, then, my mother embodied one of the modalities through which what I have called "verdicts" function: the reproduction, expressed through her, of a sentence handed down by a tribunal that sits nowhere, or rather, that sits everywhere and at all times, the stigmatization of a category of persons by way of the reiterative citation of an insulting remark, the perpetuation of a disparaging gaze.[78] But in doing this she also embodied another modality, both strange and banal, of the functioning of verdicts: their multidimensional character, the way they are always relational. She had been a *bâtarde*, an unloved illegitimate child, abandoned by her mother, someone who then became a domestic worker, sent at the age of fourteen to clean the homes of middle-class families, who went on working as a cleaning lady, then a factory worker, spending her entire life in exhausting, backbreaking work, the victim of a violent and unjust social order; she had always felt herself the subject of scorn; she had experienced endless amounts of humiliation. How, then, is it possible that she would allow herself to express at every possible moment her hatred of other stigmatized and inferiorized categories? (She always had a contribution to make to these forms of stigmatization and inferiorization, even if it was only in private. Private racism is, after all, part of what nourishes generalized racism, social racism, public racism, political racism.) She thereby affirmed her pride in being white, even if she really wasn't, given that, if I am to believe the stories she told, her biological father was a "Gypsy" from Andalusia. "Gypsy" is the word she used to speak of him, and so he was not "white"—which meant that she was not either; nor, of course, am I. This is something she never missed a chance to remind me of during my adolescence. She would say to me, for example—and it was an astonishing thing to hear her say, given that she detested those to whom she was comparing me—that I looked like a *bougnoule*.[79] "When I saw you coming down the street, for a second I thought you were a *bougnoule*." How could she at one and the same time lay claim to an ancestry that clearly positioned her on the side of nonwhites (she was both deeply saddened and shamed by this, because she had been a *bâtarde*, abandoned by her father before she was born, then by her mother while she was still a child, and also deeply proud, doubtless because of the romantic aura that her "Andalusian" or "Gypsy" roots held in her eyes) and denigrate with such aggressive language nonwhites whose skin color was simply a bit darker than hers? She had a "dark complexion," as she would put it, inherited from a parent that she deeply regretted never knowing, someone whose complexion must have been even "darker," which is to say browner, than hers.

There are many ways in which my mother was close, socially speaking, to Henry Louis Gates Jr.'s mother. His mother was a domestic worker who complained of being mistreated by the woman who employed her; she dreamed of having a house of her own but was only ever able to rent.[80] This was also true of my mother, who had done domestic work for many years and had always aspired to have her own house, without ever having the means, and who therefore spent her whole life as a renter in public housing. These two women who respond with an exclamation to analogous scenes they see on television belonged to the same social class but were separated by their skin color. What separated them won out over what they had in common.

When I reconnected with my mother after years of near-total absence, years in which we barely spoke, I was struck with compassion for this old woman suffering from so much pain. I even felt a tenderness toward her. (I'm not sure this is the right word, but I cannot find another suitable one.) This was despite everything that had driven us apart and continued to divide us. Her obsessive racism dismayed me, but in order to avoid always being in conflict, I would only protest half-heartedly when she launched into one of her habitual diatribes (herself the daughter of an immigrant) against "foreigners," who came to "our home" instead of staying "where they came from" ("It doesn't even feel like home here anymore," "They take everything and there's nothing left for us"), against "Arabs," or "Blacks," or "Chinese," all of whom she complained about endlessly. (The vocabulary she drew on to refer to all those who were the targets of her hatred was often considerably cruder and more insulting than this.) It was in part so I would no longer have to listen to this kind of talk that I had stopped seeing her and had fled from both my family and this milieu. I couldn't stand having to listen to these acrimonious tirades from one conversation to the next. Nothing had changed after all this time: on this point as on many others, she was the same as before. And yet, if I wished to spend time with her—and I did wish to, or at least it was something I felt I should do—I was going to have to accept her as she was. Nothing about her was going to change! And when I did dare to give expression to my annoyance ("Please stop saying things like that. You know I don't like it."), she would reply in a firm, almost aggressive tone: "I can say what I want in my own home. You can't tell me what to do." I had no choice but to try to understand her, to understand what she was, how and why she had become this way, and to put aside my spontaneous reactions of dismay. Am I right in thinking that, through a kind of sociopsychological alchemy, all of the social violence, the inferiorization, and the humiliation that she had suffered throughout her existence had transformed itself into an inexhaustible verbal violence against anyone she felt entitled to despise? Bourdieu has described a "law of conservation of social violence": where there has been violence, there will be more violence; people who have experienced violence will reproduce it against others. My mother's vehemence while watching television and hurling abuse at those she saw on the screen meant, I think, nothing other than this: eternally inferior, she allowed herself, through these expressions of abhorrence, the only feeling of superiority that was socially available to her—the sadly distinctive dignity of not belonging to categories so stigmatized or stigmatizable that even someone like her could ostracize and insult them. It was as if feeling herself endowed with a capacity to humiliate—even if it was only fictively, for herself alone, in speaking to the television—avenged her for having always been among the humiliated. Her verbal vehemence in these circumstances was not only painful for me to hear, but it was also difficult to understand. Why all this hatred? What slights, what wrongs had any of those people she railed against done to her? What pleasure could she take in this pointless, unjustifiable spitefulness? And if she was so angry, why was this anger not directed against other individuals, groups, or institutions, ones that bore more responsibility for the difficulties she experienced in her life than did these groups? And since, in these moments, I was the only person to hear her, the only person she was speaking to, what function did these words fulfill within her own psychic economy: Why was she saying all this to me, what irresistible need did she fulfill in manifesting her exasperation in this way in front of her television?

It is not easy to find explanations for all the unreachable depths of the social order.

5

My mother's racism frequently went beyond the limits of what I was willing to put up with in order not to fall out with her. But in truth I did not ever fall out with her. Just like the background noise of the television, this was an unpleasant circumstance that I was required to put up with while I spent time with her. Here is one example: My brother, who was living in Africa at the time, came to stay with her for a few days, along with his new partner, a woman from Guinea. As was usual, my brother and my mother spent their time together arguing, quite vehemently for the most part. It is always surprising, I might add in passing, to see how a family that presents itself as tightly knit together by "family feeling" actually functions. It was this same brother, in fact, who reacted with such violence upon reading *Returning to Reims*. He sent me a long and insulting message, telling me I did not understand what a family truly was and that I was about to find out once all my brothers banded together against me—a suggestion that obviously carried with it a familiar and unpleasant whiff of homophobia. He threatened me with a lawsuit for "family calumny," which made my attorney smile when I told him about it. There is no such thing, legally speaking. In any case, neither my mother nor my other two brothers had any interest in joining with him in taking any such step. Each time that he would arrive at my mother's, things would become tense, and arguments, including regular shouting matches, became one of the major modes of their interactions. This is just what used to happen any time he ended up in the same room with my father or my older brother: The situation would immediately become tense, to such an extent that they would sometimes come to blows. My mother would be yelling at them, as if it were a scene in some neorealist Italian film (it was she who described the scene to me): "Don't get up to that here, you'll break everything. Go fight outside." Which they would do. (Édouard Louis describes a similar scene between his brother and his father in *Who Killed My Father*.) My brother is bad-tempered, irascible, and most importantly, he has interiorized to such a degree the idea that men shouldn't have to perform any kind of domestic labor that on this occasion he had asked my mother: "Where's the laundry you did this morning?" She had replied: "It's still in the machine." He blew up: "Why couldn't you take it out and hang it up to dry?" His partner, who was pregnant, was there resting on the sofa. That is when my mother pointed at her and made this ghastly reply: "What about her? You couldn't tell her to do it? The world is really upside down now if white people have to work for Black people."

When she recounted this scene to me over the telephone, her voice still quivering with indignation, yet proud of how she had reacted (she wanted to show me that she didn't let herself be pushed around, a theme that frequently recurred in the anecdotes she would tell me in which she was always playing a role that enhanced her status), I was so dumbstruck that I thought at first she must be exaggerating: "You didn't really say that, did you?" Indeed, she had. She insisted on it, repeating the odious sentence to me two or three times: she really had said it. So I said to her: "Maman, you can't say things like that." To which she replied: "I'm someone who has a hard time walking, and there she is lying on the sofa, lounging like a princess, and I'm the one who's supposed to hang up the laundry?" I responded: "But instead of insulting his wife, you should have told that idiot of a son of yours to take his own laundry out of the machine."

Here again we see that strange imbrication of incorporated forms of social domination: my brother, so attached to the demands of a conventionally defined masculinity, unable to let go of them for even a brief second; my mother, old and physically diminished, but finding no other way of opposing the stupidity of his ableist and masculinist stance than through the stupidity of her own racism… It is hard for me to find the words to describe how despondent all these conversations left me. From the time I became a student I had set up my life so that I would no longer have to be confronted by these kinds of statements, ones I had heard day in and day out during my childhood and my adolescence. Yet here they were again, more violent than they had ever been, and I couldn't avoid them. My mother was a racist old woman, and I had no choice but to accept her as such.

I am filled with sadness and shame again as I describe these scenes, ones that occurred regularly throughout all the stages of my mother's slow decline. And yet it is necessary that I do so. I don't wish to paint illuminations, edifying scenes, but rather a realist picture. Even if her displays of racism became more severe as the years went by, the racism itself cannot be ascribed to her extreme age. It had always been there, as far back as I can remember. I also remember that she was able to express this racism with no fear of being contradicted: it would always be met with agreement by those who heard what she said, for the simple reason that they shared her feelings. It seemed to bring the community of white workers together in their relation to the world and to others.

This also means that when, in the 1970s or 1980s, she would participate in a strike, when she would follow a union's directive, when she would be a worker taking part in a mobilization, and when, in a certain way, she would thereby inscribe herself into the long history of the workers' movement—a history composed not only of major events that mark the history of the "class struggle in France," as Marx would say, but also of more modest acts of resistance and daily interventions—at the same time she would be the same racist woman she had always been and would never cease being, even if at such moments it didn't express itself, or did so to a lesser degree. Strikes or other organized political activities had a dampening effect on the expression of racist feelings. When you support a strike or a movement, you are necessarily situated on the side of your fellow strikers, those who work to resist as best they can the violence of exploitation; you are one of those who bring into existence the movement or the mobilization. Yet this does not necessarily mean that you adhere to everything all these people think, say, and feel individually (or even collectively, really). We need to break with the mythology of the working class that still shades many people's perceptions—both on the left and on the right—regarding workers who are the salt of the earth, "good people," "healthy," "moral," and "decent" (this is the version on the right or the extreme right), or the heroic proletariat, with "men of steel" and "mother courage" figures fighting for the working class, people with a spontaneous consciousness of the reality of their oppression, and to whom no flaws or failings can be imputed unless you wish to be accused of being reactionary or bourgeois (this is the version on the left). To speak of the racism and homophobia that are so strongly present, that saturate the working classes, is to run the risk of being accused of "class elitism" or "prolophobia." People will object to you that "middle-class people are also racist and homophobic," as if that were a serious objection when addressed to an author who is describing the environment of their own childhood and adolescence, who is not from a middle-class background, or when addressed to someone who is describing the kinds of things their mother said throughout her life. Are you supposed to keep hidden what you saw, heard, and lived through, simply because similar discriminatory impulses also exist in other social spaces? To say that racism and homophobia exist in working-class environments is not to say that they do not also exist elsewhere. It is simply to say that they exist in working-class environments.

I could add ten, twenty, or a hundred more conversations such as the ones I have just described… Even when my mother was trying to convince me that she was not racist, she was being racist. One day, speaking about her newest grandchild (the son of my brother and of his wife whom my mother had insulted a few years earlier), she said: "He's Black, but I think of him the same way as I think of my other grandchildren; I don't treat him differently." Or there was the time when she needed to find a new doctor closer to home once she had moved back to Reims. I asked her, "Did you like your new doctor?" "Yes, I was shocked when I opened the door because, well, you know, he was Black… But I liked him fine." "But Maman, I didn't ask you if he was Black or white; I asked if you liked him." She responded in that half-stubborn, half-mocking tone of a little old lady that she found it convenient to adopt whenever she didn't feel like arguing but also didn't want to concede any ground: "Yes, yes, yes, I just said I liked him fine… But still… It seemed a little strange to me…"

Once when she was still able to travel and she was on her way to visit my brother in the South of France, she needed to switch from one train station to another in Paris. She got on the commuter train going in the wrong direction and found herself in the suburbs. That meant getting off the train and asking directions of the travelers waiting on the platform, who explained what she needed to do. "I was a little worried," she said to me, "because there were only Black people, but they were all very nice." I then asked her: "But Maman, why wouldn't they have been nice to you?" She replied, "Oh, you know, what with everything you see on TV!" Watching television all day also meant absorbing a stream of biased images that nourished and reinforced her already hostile dispositions to a world she barely knew (Parisian commuter trains, and the people who lived in the towns on the outskirts of Paris).

Still, I have to admit that, in spite of all these unpleasant episodes, watching television also served as a way of spending time together without having to find new topics of conversation once we had covered the usual health issues, family matters, a few memories, a few anecdotes (either new ones or ones repeated for the hundredth time). The two of us could sit there without talking or simply trading a few words about the images passing on the screen in front of us (a science documentary, or a historical or geographical one, or one about animals, or a retrospective look at this or that variety show artist). After all, being together, being right next to each other, without saying anything, is also one of the privileged ways of relating to those we are close to (especially to those we are closest to among our close relations), because it requires a heightened degree of intimacy or of closeness. There was no need for me to make any attempt to keep the conversation going. We were fine like that. This way of being together also had the advantage of avoiding strained moments.

She was passionate about Formula 1 racing and could spend hours following along as the racing cars went round and round the track. She kept her eyes glued to the television screen and seemed so fascinated that it was as if she almost forgot I was there. I expressed my surprise: "You really find this so fascinating?" She replied: "Oh, yes! I would have loved to be a race car driver!" I pointed out: "I don't think there are many women drivers, and there would have been even fewer back in your day." She would shrug her shoulders and laugh: "I know that, but even so..." Yes, even so—even if there had been women drivers, they wouldn't have been women from the working classes. This is a particularly expensive sport, exclusively for rich people, for the very rich.

She could only dream of all the possibilities that had not been hers, of all the roads that had been closed to the impoverished young woman she had been, roads that she probably never gave a thought to taking at the time because they were excluded from her social—and therefore her mental—horizon. She had never imagined becoming a judge, a lawyer, a doctor, an engineer, or an architect, professions that were mostly inaccessible to women in those days and totally closed to the working classes—something (as far as the working class goes) that has scarcely changed today—but she would have liked to become a teacher. Even that hope proved unrealistic, or in any case proved impossible to realize. So if you were going to dream, especially if you were going to dream retrospectively, why not dream of the most improbable things, the most impossible ones, given that none of them had been seriously envisaged, or indeed had been seriously envisageable. In any case, none of them would ever have come about: to become a Formula 1 driver, or to become an airplane pilot, as she sometimes mentioned, was, when you thought about it, hardly any less realistic than imagining yourself in some other profession. Yet out of this huge ocean of impossible things, out of all the unenvisageable things that made up her life, which had been given over to necessity and not to choice, at least these dreams had the advantage of allowing her the freedom to roam about in a place where her most flamboyant, crazy schemes could be freely developed. She could project herself into the image of the free, independent, daring woman that she had so wished she could be, had the social world been other than what it was (and what it still is), had she not been a domestic worker who at twenty married a factory worker on the lowest rung of the working ladder. It is an immutable law of human existence: you cannot wipe out the past. It was what it was. The most that you can do is to transform its meaning by way of your present situation and by the way you project yourself into the future. (I am well aware of what a Sartrean/Beauvoirian kind of phrase that is.) For that, too, it would be necessary for the present and the future to be dimensions in which some form of change was possible. For my mother, given her age, given her physical condition, it was not in the real world that the meaning of her past was going to change.

Her physical and social conditions came together and reinforced each other to enhance the impossibility of what had always been impossible, or rather to render that impossibility immutable and definitive. People often cite Malraux's phrase from *Man's Hope*: "The terrible thing about death is that it transforms life into destiny." Could not something almost identical be said about very old age, the stage at which life closes in on itself and little by little transforms itself into destiny? So it is that the television could serve as a dream machine, or perhaps better, as a machine producing fantasies that allow for the suspension in your mind of the distinction between what is real and what is imaginary, what is true and what is false, what is past and what is present; a machine that need pay no heed to the implacable determinisms of class, gender, and age… It erased destiny, the irrevocability of the established meaning of a given existence. Because she could no longer project herself into the future, she projected herself into an imaginary past: another past became possible and this meant other lives were possible, other experiences, other sensations. She let herself be transported into other situations, into other worlds—worlds to which the mediation of the television screen could give her access for a brief moment. And yet, since in any case she almost never left the house anymore, that was enough for her. No longer having any social connections, no longer having an active life, more and more cut off from anyone and everyone around her, she took refuge in the frenetic ballet of race cars, and she followed it fervently and with passion. Motionless in her armchair, with the remote control in her hand, she was behind the wheel of a race car.

6

My mother read the regional newspaper on a daily basis. She devoured all the local news, read all the different sections, including "health and beauty," "cooking," "advice," "interior design," "gardening and home improvements" (even if she had no garden and made no improvements), and "travel" (even though she hadn't taken any trips in years). Still, we probably all read pages in the newspaper that have no immediate usefulness for us; we probably all enjoy reading travel and tourism supplements, with photos and suggestions for things to see and recommendations for hotels and restaurants that we know we will never visit. She was a subscriber, and what she called "my newspaper" was delivered to her mailbox. There came a time when she decided the subscription was too expensive for her and so she asked to be sent the newspaper only every other day. I offered to pay for her subscription, since it was so important to her that she be able to read "her" newspaper every morning, but she absolutely refused. "It's not something you should be paying for." I insisted, but she would not reconsider. She also read cheesy novels, printed in big type, romances. The covers always had sensual (heterosexual) scenes on them, where a handsome young man embraced an equally young and beautiful woman, suggesting that the plot would be more than simply sentimental. I wondered where she got them from. I had no idea where one went to buy books of this kind. (In the notebook where I kept my notes in preparation for writing this volume, I jotted down: "Talk about the novel she read. No idea where she got them from.") Why didn't I ever ask her? It remained a mystery for me until the day when, well after she had died, I found the answer: I saw the same books—exactly the same ones—in the hands of the actress who was playing Annie Ernaux in the film adaptation of one of her novels: she is buying a couple of these books in a supermarket near where she lives, giving up on demanding literature in order to enjoy stereotypical descriptions of sentimental and sexual passions.[81] When, out of curiosity, I picked one of these volumes up off of the coffee table in front of her sofa, my mother said, with a forced laugh, as if worried I was going to judge her somehow: "Leave that be, it's not a book for you… I know it's nonsense… But I enjoy that kind of thing." I would in fact be interested in reading one or two of them today, just to find out what kind of "nonsense" they contain. Yet where am I going to buy them, since I never find myself in the kind of supermarket I now know she went to in order to do her shopping—that is, when she was still able to get about?[82]

There was a day when, looking in a small fake-antique wooden cabinet (a style she liked) for a document she had asked me to find, I saw, in the middle of a row of these novels that she so enjoyed, and that she kept once she finished reading them, a few old books of mine that I must have left behind with some other belongings when I moved out of the family apartment at the age of nineteen and wasn't able to take everything with me. There was Camus's *The Stranger* alongside Sartre's *The Words* in the Gallimard paperback editions, and also two volumes from the Maspero pocketbook collection that contained Marx and Engels's writings on syndicalism.[83] "Hey, those belong to me!" I exclaimed. She looked at them and replied, "Huh, well, of course. I mean, obviously I don't read that kind of stuff." And when I added, "Can I take them?" she looked at me with amusement and said: "Sure, they're yours. What am I going to do with them?"

These conversations we had that may have seemed banal were saturated with social and cultural meanings. Juxtaposed in the way they were, those books in her apartment, hers from today, mine from long ago, existed in direct opposition to each other. The two volumes of Marx and Engels left behind in the apartment in the low-income housing complex where we lived while I was a teenager, with their very plain covers, one red, the other purple, had been printed in January 1972. (The print run of the first printing is indicated at the back of the volume: 15,000 copies, which is quite impressive and shows the degree of interest in this kind of publication at the time.) I had therefore bought them shortly before leaving my family to move into a small room in the center of town, the first step in my "flight," one which would quickly lead me to Paris. Despite their slightly faded colors, these volumes shone rather brightly as symbols of the gap that had already formed itself at that earlier moment. Lying there on the table, they represented the cultural distance that had started to grow between us and that would turn into an ever-greater social distance in the years that followed. (Yet even back then it had already become a social distance, since my parents were factory workers, whereas I was a student.)

My mother had a very strong feeling of the cultural illegitimacy of the kinds of things she read and of her own taste for this kind of literature, a feeling that she expressed, before I had said the slightest thing on the topic, by declaring to me that the books she read weren't my kind of books, and that she knew quite well that they were "nonsense," or, conversely, by telling me that those volumes by Marx and Engels were not for her. She had never read, and would never have been able to read, works of that kind. She left school at the age of fourteen and so didn't have the necessary educational background. She had not been able to acquire either the cultural or the intellectual "disposition" that would have allowed her to be interested in what interested me—literary classics, for example, or works on syndicalism. It goes without saying that, as was the case for Marx and Engels, she had never opened, and never would open, the Camus novel or the Sartre autobiography... She lacked the scholarly and cultural "competence" for that, something that is neither universal nor inborn, but rather something that is acquired in the dominant classes starting in childhood, as a class privilege, by way of the family transmission and the social transmission of cultural capital, and then by time spent in certain tracks within the educational system (the ones that are not directed specifically toward apprenticeships in manual and technical forms of labor). Neither my father nor my mother, nor anyone else in my family, read Marx. It is hardly worth dwelling on this, since it seems so obvious.

The volumes I found in that cabinet so many years later and that I put on the table next to the ones my mother was reading represented this impassable paradox: she was the one who had worked in a factory; I was the one interested in the history of the workers' movement, in the theory of syndicalism. (In 1972 she was already working in a factory, and I had just started at the university.) And the required condition for my interest in the theory of syndicalism, in the sociology of class, in political philosophy had been that I leave behind the working-class world of my childhood, the one in which my mother remained immersed. Because she had been a worker, she read "nonsense"; because I had not been, I had read Marx, then Sartre, then Bourdieu…

If they stood there as signs of the distance that had grown up between us, the volumes of Marx and Engels held, at the same time, and just as significantly, an opposite meaning: an intellectual and political fidelity to the working-class world that I came from. As I read Marx in those years, as I aligned myself politically with the working class at the same time as I was (socially and culturally) leaving it behind, I was joining together with my mother and my family, even though I could no longer live with them. This was my way of not betraying them at the outset of my trajectory as a class renegade, a trajectory that does always and inevitably imply a certain betrayal. (So many authors have written about this question that it could become a topic for a thesis or anthology: "The Theme of Betrayal in the Writings of Class Renegades.") But from this point of view, from the political point of view, I can affirm that I have never betrayed them.

Each time that I came to see her at her home, whether it was in Muizon or later in Tinqueux, before she was admitted to the nursing home, I could tell that she had hardly any interest in politics, or in what politics meant to me. What she did react to were more human-interest stories found in the popular press, or sensational news items: "Did you see? Something really bad happened," she told me in a shaky voice just after she opened the door one day on my arrival. "No, what?" I asked. "You didn't hear? The bus of tourists that flipped over in a ditch. People died." Her day was punctuated by the news bulletins brought to her on television: sensational stories, traffic accidents, celebrity gossip… The local newspaper also provided plenty of occasions for her to get riled up, to become indignant, and sometimes (more rarely) to rejoice. Small local stories about a burglary, an assault, or a crime committed in town, episodes of extreme bad weather, all took on more importance in her eyes than anything that might be taking place internationally or in some far-off country. Even things happening in nearby nations, I might add, held no interest for her. "Sensationalism attracts notice," Bourdieu emphasized in *On Television*, "and it also diverts it" (Mais les faits divers, ce sont aussi des faits qui font diversion.)[84] Every time I went to visit my mother, I couldn't help but think how correct this observation was. All these "breaking news" items that came to her through this permanent filter—the reality of the world as intercepted and filtered by the media—triggered reactions in her that drew almost exclusively on an affective register. She would pass without pause from compassion to anger, from distress to fury, and she would express her feelings with an emotional intensity or a linguistic vehemence that never ceased to astonish me. After all, that is probably the effect that is sought after and achieved by those who activate this filter and make it work: engage people's affects—above all negative ones, ones having to do with resentment—and orient them toward sensational stories in order to disengage any possible interest they might have for more essential and more "political" (in the larger sense of the term) issues.

My mother always voted. Or almost always. When she abstained, it was not out of indifference, but as a deliberate and collective gesture of defiance and rejection. Speaking to me one day about Muizon, the village she was then living in, she said: "I'm not voting tomorrow. No one goes to vote here, everyone abstains.

We're sick of it all." This refusal to participate—a phenomenon that has only increased since then—is a way of expressing an opinion: not only that you do not recognize yourself in any of the candidates that you have to choose from, but also that you do not recognize yourself as part of the electoral process itself. So you choose not to play the game; you stay on the sidelines. Was it because of her age, which is to say the generation she was part of (she was fifteen when women gained the right to vote), that this withdrawal was never a permanent one for her? In any case, she did vote again in the next election.

Since she no longer had any attachment to collective frameworks for working out a political position, since she had so few contacts with the external world, she would choose between candidates based on varying kinds of criteria that were sometimes difficult to understand. She voted for Jean-Marie Le Pen because she wanted to "teach them a lesson," at a moment when voting for the National Front started to take root and to thrive in the heart of what used to be the "working class." Then she voted for the extremely reactionary Sarkozy against the Socialist Ségolène Royal (whom she particularly detested), then for Sarkozy again against the Socialist Hollande (I am not absolutely sure of that one), and finally, in the first round, for Macron, a former investment banker, even though he stood for everything she had risen up against twenty or thirty years earlier. Her argument for this, when I objected, was disconcerting: "I know all that, but he's young." Or, even more absurdly: "Yes, but he's handsome." This was a choice she soon bitterly regretted, ranting about this neoliberal and authoritarian political figure soon after his election, when he had barely had time to announce the first of his measures to cut the social welfare system, making clear that she should have voted for Marine Le Pen, and that she would do so the next time around.

It has to be said that she had arrived at a point where any and everything that sounded "leftish" or that had to do with "the Left" was utterly detestable to her. As a rule, she was prepared to vote for almost anyone as long as they were opposed to the Left. She therefore often voted for candidates on the right or the extreme right in municipal, regional, and European elections, as well as in legislative and presidential ones (with only a few exceptions that I have trouble identifying and explaining).

The man she was so taken with, another former factory worker, was even further to the right than she was. He seemed authentically fascist to me—and that is speaking euphemistically—when he showed up one day in the middle of one of my visits to my mother and let out: "Nothing works in this country any more… What we need is a new Hitler." I turned to look at him. He was smiling contentedly. He seemed happy with what he had said. Is it really what he thought, or was he trying to get under the skin of a leftist, Parisian intellectual—which is what I was for him, someone who represented everything he despised: Paris, "elites," the "system," the Left? I decided not to react and so made no effort to understand what he meant. I pretended I hadn't understood what he had said and asked my mother some unrelated question, something like "What time is your nurse coming tomorrow?" or some other banal question that habitually served the purpose of changing the topic of the conversation when I could no longer bear remarks that were racist or politically painful for me—remarks of a kind that she addressed to me endlessly and that, apparently, she could not or would not resist making to me. Was not what I was witnessing there, in real time, in front of me, in her home, the spectacle of the disintegration of a social class, and of the "class consciousness" she was supposed to incarnate? And that in fact she had incarnated in the past. There I was in my mother's living room, and because it was my mother's living room, I was with a woman who was racist and a man who was a neofascist or even pro-Nazi, both of them former factory workers, people who had, in the past, represented voters of the Left, the social base of leftist parties.

My mother's relation to politics, or, more exactly, her interest in politics, did not seem to go beyond this electoral dimension to which she attached so much importance. Had she been more politically engaged when she was younger? Obviously, she hadn't been during the period when she was a cleaning woman and therefore isolated due to the fact that she worked on her own. (She worked in private homes, not in offices or large hotels with other wage earners, and therefore she wasn't able to be part of a union or to engage in political activities: With whom and against whom would she have done so? She did not rise up against her employers who, she thought, treated her well, generally speaking. I am even convinced that she had an affair with one of them, because I remember that she would leave us, me and my brother, young children at the time, in the backyard on those days when we didn't have school and she brought us with her to work. She would ask us to stay outside, and then disappear into the house for an hour or so.) But she certainly was politically engaged once she became a worker. During that period, she could always be counted on to follow a call to strike, or to take part in a work stoppage or an assembly in front of the factory. She would sometimes speak scornfully about her fellow workers, many of whom would loudly express their support when the union delegate called a meeting at the entry gates for the next morning when a stoppage or a protest action was scheduled, but then who would show up in much smaller numbers the next day. "It works like this: when it's just words, everyone's willing, but when it comes to showing up, no one's there! A bunch of cowards." She lived in a politicized world, given that everyone in her family—her brother and his wife, my father, his brothers and sisters…—all claimed to be leftists. Moreover, as part of "the Left," they thought of themselves as belonging to a world of "workers" in the economic and class-based meaning of the word, but also in the political sense. "We, the workers" was a political category, a way of naming how you saw yourself politically. In the 1960s, people spoke disparagingly of Harold Wilson and the Labourite left in the UK, who simply wanted to reform the system (by way, it must be said, of a platform and a project that would appear to today's mainstream media, in the UK, in France, and across Europe, as "radical" and "extremist"). In the 1970s, people would repeat over and over: "For us it's the Programme commun!" by which they meant the electoral agreement that the Communist Party had signed with the Socialist Party, despite the great mistrust in which the Socialists were held. It was understood that they were always ready and willing to betray the working class…

In 1981, my mother would make fun of those of her colleagues at the factory who, too susceptible to media and political propaganda, were worried about what a victory of the Left in the presidential election would mean: "If Mitterrand wins, they'll take away our houses." The state's policy of expanding the availability of bank loans and encouraging people to aim for "individual houses" (taking on debt for twenty-five or thirty years) meant that many workers' households (and it was more true for women—less politicized and less engaged with the union—than for men) were more receptive to the Right's denunciation of the specter of "socialist collectivism," and they really imagined that a leftist government's first action would be to seize their tiny individual homes that were of such poor quality. "You can't believe how stupid those women are," my mother would say about her colleagues at work. In any case, this aspiration toward individuation (a house), and to the private happiness that was associated with it, contributed to the disintegration of the idea of a collectivity, and to the feeling of belonging to such a "collective," one that deserved and still deserves to be called a "class," the "working class." All of these phenomena would become more pronounced in the years and decades that followed.

Still, my mother couldn't help feeing a certain mistrust for unions as well, or at least for the union activists. "They just like telling everyone else what to do," while knowing that "they don't risk anything themselves" and that "other people take the risks for them." Or else, "They're just doing it to get ahead at work." And it is true that there is no shortage of examples of highly active union delegates who ended up being neutralized by way of a promotion within the workplace. "He sold out," "They bought him off," as people used to say. (It happened to one of my uncles, who was thereafter judged quite severely and scornfully by everyone else in the family, even if the judgment might be slightly softened by way of a few understanding comments. Yes, he was a "traitor" who "went over to the boss's side," but given that he was looking to better his situation, were you going to throw the first stone?)

This "class consciousness," or perhaps, something that is not exactly the same thing, this consciousness of oneself as belonging to a class ("we the workers"), as sharing a set of working conditions and common interests that are linked to those common conditions, was grounded both in the material frameworks of existence (the factory, the neighborhood) and in the forms of organization that gave meaning to these situations: the unions, the party… (for even if one didn't belong to the party, still its perspectives and its way of representing things were known to everyone, and provided ways of thinking about oneself). *Solidarity* is not a vain word. I remember well how, in May and June of 1968, one of my father's sisters and her husband came for dinner at my parents' home, along with other members of the family. They were active in the movement and had lost their pay. My mother made huge omelets. It was her way of contributing to the strike. (She wasn't a worker yet and I do not know how she managed to find the means—however slight for these very simple meals—to feed all these people on strike.) My uncle, a Communist worker, took me to the huge demonstrations in which people marched regularly through the center of town in those days. These were the first protests I ever attended. I started young.

The factory where my mother worked in the 1970s and 1980s employed seventeen hundred men and women as workers, five hundred of whom belonged to the CGT, the union closest in those days to the powerful Communist Party. (People said that it was the "drive belt" of the party.) There were others who supported or belonged to other unions. This represented a considerable strength, when people were mobilized for the long term, and they could be mobilized whenever the occasion called for it. A strike broke out in 1977 to obtain a guaranteed bonus, improvements in working conditions, and the rehiring of two workers who had been fired for distributing political tracts at the factory gate. The atmosphere between employers and the workers' unions in the region had become tense since Reims had elected a Communist mayor in the last municipal elections at the beginning of the year. Massive numbers of workers went out on strike, with a picket line in front of the factory's locked gates. One night some members of a private militia (part of a small right-wing union from another factory with ties to the bosses) drove by in a car and fired some shots at the union members who were there. One of them didn't survive. My mother had a strong memory of this dramatic moment. She was one of the strikers, even though she wasn't present at the moment of the shooting. (There probably weren't many women in the groups who picketed at night.) Workers were intensely engaged at the time, and the forces of repression did whatever they could to break their will. After this murder, there were stoppages and protests in solidarity all over town, and thousands of people attended the funeral of the worker who had been killed.[85]

Ten years later, the factory was not doing well; it would soon go under. The number of people who worked there was declining. This was the case as well in the other large glass works in town, as in most of the factories throughout the region. This meant there were layoffs or, as in the case of my mother, people given early retirement; there were workers who were partially unemployed, and others fully unemployed and looking for work… Then the factory closed. That was quite a while ago, but the buildings are still there: empty, abandoned, run-down. They provide evidence of these kinds of workplaces that seemed straight out of the nineteenth century, of the violence of capitalism, of the hardship of these kinds of employment. But they also serve as examples of the kinds of spaces of organized resistance that existed.

Where are the workers now? For the most part, they have died. What about their children and grandchildren? Most likely, when they aren't stuck in long periods of unemployment, they work in temporary, precarious forms of employment. They will be employed in various positions having to do with logistics, in the warehouses in which a new working class is forming, one in which people work in exhausting conditions and under permanent surveillance. Where are the CGT union cards? What happened to the collective strength that one saw in my mother's generation?

I went to visit the factory again shortly before my mother's death. The outside walls were covered in graffiti and posters for the National Front. Everything inside gave an impression of desolation. The windows were broken, the ground was covered with broken bottles and shards of glass... There were orange-red rubber washers everywhere, the ones that would have been used on the jars to which workers attached the circles of metal that held the covers in place... In the midst of this scene of ruin I reflected on what my mother's existence had been, on the world she had belonged to. I thought of the oppressive heat that would assault all the bodies working there—from the manufacturing furnaces, of course—filling these spaces that were now empty and windswept; I thought of the infernal noise, as well, of the harshness of all of these kinds of jobs, of the danger caused by the dust from the materials in use, of all the workplace injuries, many of them extremely serious ones... I thought of those days gone by. Then I thought of the nursing home awaiting her, the one I was about to help her move into. "There it is," I said to myself: "That's what the life of a working-class woman was, and that's what her old age is." I didn't expect that I would have to add a third word to the list quite so soon.

• We always lived in public housing. When I was a child, public employees would come through the buildings every month to collect the rent and perhaps also, although here my memory isn't so clear, the gas and electricity payments. It would often be the case that my mother (for this kind of task always fell to women to manage) was unable to pay. We were frequently short on money, and it was a challenge to meet these payment deadlines. As the lovely French expression goes, we had to *tirer le diable par la queue*, to "pull the devil by his tail," to scrape by, to live from hand to mouth. It was an expression my mother used often; the reality it referred to was not lovely at all. As the day approached, my mother would keep a lookout for the housing employee or the electricity worker, and when she saw him in the street, she would shut herself into her bedroom, doing her best not to make any noise. She told us not to open the door when he rang, but to say from inside "Maman isn't home." The scene might repeat itself for a few days running, as well as from month to month.

• She was still very young (fifteen or sixteen) when a woman she worked for doing housework, someone kinder and more generous than the others, paid for her to take some shorthand and typing classes so that she could become a secretary. It represented an amazing possibility for her. "I was good at it," she told me. But the bureaucracy in charge of finding a "place" for these young girls once they left the "charitable institution" (the institution that took in orphans and abandoned children until they reached the age of fourteen) never left them long with the same employer; it was always moving them quickly to someone new. She had to give up her classes, and never became a secretary. She remained a girl who did housework and then became a cleaning lady.

• Before the start of each school year, when it was time for new "school clothes" for me and my older brother, my mother would take us with her for what was a kind of end-of-summer ritual there was no way of getting out of: in an alley located between two middle-class streets in the center of the city, where things could happen more or less out of sight, she would take out a "loan" that allowed her to buy all the clothes we needed. She would pay this "loan" back over many months at, I imagine, an extremely high rate of interest. What choice did she have? Being poor is expensive. When we would ask for more than what her budget could cover with the loan she had taken out, she would get angry with us: "Stop always asking for more… I'm only buying things for you, nothing for me… Be happy with what you get." It's true that she never spent much on her own clothes, and that throughout her whole life she "counted her pennies." She only rarely bought her clothes in the department stores in the center of town. For the most part, she thought they were too expensive for her and so she would usually go to shops closer to where we lived. She would often order skirts, blouses, and sweaters for herself, along with trousers and shirts for my father from the catalogs of a mail-order company. (It was called, and still is, I think, La Redoute à Roubaix, a name that came up frequently in family conversations, because everyone would order things from La Redoute à Roubaix.)

• I have other memories of her and her moments of anger. This one is from before she began working in the factory. I must have been fourteen or fifteen years old. She had found an odd job, to bring in a bit of money: putting publicity flyers into mailboxes. She was assigned a neighborhood and given a huge bundle of papers, and off she went, carrying a bag much too heavy for her, to put the flyers one by one in mailboxes, street by street, house by house, building by building. She would force me to go with her and help when I didn't have school. It was obviously something I hated doing. (Just as it was obviously something she hated doing even more than I did.) There was one day when the neighborhood she had been assigned was close to my high school. I was horrified at the idea that some students, a classmate, or a teacher might see me and recognize me... My entire body, my entire being wanted nothing to do with the whole situation: shame, basically, social shame was there in me prior to any actual gaze, anticipating it, fearing it. I tried to make myself as small as possible, to be as close to invisible as possible, so that I might avoid this potential "gaze" that I found so threatening. We had the habit of dividing the assigned streets between us to be more efficient, and so I took advantage of a moment when she couldn't see me to throw a huge stack of the flyers into a trash can. A few moments later, when she had figured out what I had done, she went into one of those fits of rage that were so familiar with her: "I'll lose this job because of you. Then where will the food to feed you come from? Where will the money come from to send you to your high school?" Her words were a bit more colorful, a bit cruder. But if I cited here the precise language she used back then, I would be accused of deriding working-class forms of speech. Yet if I wanted to give a more precise description of the language she used, I would have no choice.

In any case, I was overwhelmed by that kind of shame that consists in the fear of being discovered and then judged, made fun of (at least that is what I imagined would happen). I was truly ashamed: of myself, of her, of what we were, of what we were obliged to do. One day, it was so cold outside that we put on woolen gloves whose fingertips we had cut off so that we could still separate the individual sheets from one another. It was shame about a kind of poverty that none of my classmates lived in or experienced. When I think back over these episodes in our lives, remembering her becoming angry with me on one of these mornings or afternoons when we were to go out together to distribute the flyers, when it would be obvious that I didn't want to go with her, that I was unhappy at having to do so, it now seems flagrantly obvious to me that she must have felt hurt: I was aspiring to be something else, and she was condemned to these kinds of tasks. Our verbal confrontations were a manifestation of the fact that a gap between us had already begun to establish itself. She was a prisoner for life in a reality no one could wish for, whereas I was dreaming of other things, of leaving, of making an escape. She understood all of this. Or she could at least sense what was happening. This only increased her bitterness. She was passing out these flyers so that I could get away from her. And I was trying to avoid distributing them because I wanted to be in my room reading, because I had already put some distance between us, between me and them, my family, my surroundings, all of which I needed to leave behind in order to become someone else.[86]

This kind of work was hard on her shoulders and on her back. Things would be even worse at the factory. Her body suffered throughout her entire working life, up to the moment she retired.

• Something similar happened during one summer vacation when I was employed at the same factory where my mother worked, just before I started at the university. I was, as is indicated on the pay stub that I recently came across, an "unskilled laborer." Along with another temporarily employed student, my job consisted, for example, in unloading wooden pallets from a truck so they could be taken into the workshops. One day when it was quite hot and we had finished unloading the truck, I leaned up against a wall to catch my breath for a moment. A foreman appeared within a second to shout: "What do you think you are doing? Get back to work! On the double!"

I snapped back: "We aren't slaves. We have the right to rest for a couple of minutes." He took me to the personnel office, and I was immediately let go. They paid me what I was owed for the four weeks that had already gone by. (I was supposed to work for a month and a half.) I was proud of myself. I had talked back to one of the "boss's cops," as I said at the time, whose job it was to keep an eye on the workers and keep them under control. It must have been an unusual experience for him. He had seemed utterly taken aback by my attitude, in fact. When my mother learned what had happened later that evening, she couldn't hide how angry she was. Far from being amused or happy that I had found a way to resist the brutality of one of the horrid little bosses whose job it was to keep an eye on the pace of the production line, to regulate the movements and gestures of the women working on it, she was instead worried by what had happened: "What if I lose my job because of you?" But I saw that what she was expressing was above all a sense of injustice: she could never allow herself to reply to a foreman in the way I had. In a factory you do as you are told or you are shown the door. She had to hold her tongue, even when she wanted to rebel against the working conditions that were destroying her body. She spent more than fifteen years in this factory, which means that for more than fifteen years she was obliged to repress her own reactions in order to "keep her job."

• On one visit back to see my parents in the housing complex that they were still living in north of the city, for some occasion or other (her birthday?) not long after I had left, during the period when I was still coming back to visit from time to time, I gave her a bottle of Shalimar by Guerlain. What a ridiculous idea! She worked in a factory and never wore this kind of high-end perfume. I found the bottle a few months later on a shelf somewhere. It had never been opened. She bought more affordable kinds of *eau de toilette* and had turned her nose up at this present, which must have seemed bizarre to her. Had she seen in it a surreptitious way of pointing to the class difference that was emerging between us? That had obviously not been my intention (at least not consciously). But as I think back on it, and see in my mind this Guerlain bottle in the closet where the trash chutes were found (those contraptions that could be found in buildings like theirs, by way of which you could send all your garbage directly down to the bins in the basement), I wonder if, by offering her such an expensive perfume, I had not, under the pretext of making her happy, been trying to find a way of imagining her moving into a world that was not hers—and that was not mine either. I wonder if she had simply set aside my gesture, without even having to think about it, without making any kind of decision. (I find it bizarre how today all of this, which seems to me as self-evident as it is elusive or undefinable, becomes false as soon as I write it down. It has to do more with a "je ne sais quoi" or something that is "next to nothing" and that writing cannot capture. It seems important to make the effort to reconstruct it, and yet I cannot manage to do so.)

• One night when he had had too much to drink, my father, who got around by moped, had crashed into a stationary truck. While he wasn't hurt badly, he was still required to appear before a judge. I'm not sure what his sentence was. It was probably just a fine. But I remember this: his civic rights were to be suspended for two years, which meant he could not vote during that period of time. My mother's reaction, so typical of the relation that the working classes had to institutions and to politics, was to say, "If it was me, when I got my rights back, I'd still never vote again." In her eyes, the judge and the judicial system's decision in the case of a traffic accident, politics and elections—they were all the same thing, part of the same system (one that could be called the power of the dominant classes, the powerful people, over the dominated, people like her, like us). As I write these lines, I find myself wondering, when you really think about it, if she was not right to look at it in this way. But in any case, since she was not the person who had been sanctioned in this instance, she continued voting as she had always done.

• When I was fourteen, I wanted to buy a large black umbrella. It was a way of being different, because men, in the milieu to which I still belonged, never carried umbrellas. It went against the rules of masculinity. Women (my mother, my aunts) had collapsible umbrellas in bright colors (red, pink, orange, light blue, green…) that most of the time they kept in their purses.

When it rained, I took the bus to get to the high school. (I had to transfer in the city center, because we lived on the periphery, and it was a long route.) Otherwise, weather permitting, I went by bicycle for the first few years and then by VéloSoleX, a motorized bicycle that was quite distinctive and identified me as someone going to high school. Young workers and apprentices in the neighborhood had mopeds. Taking the bus when it rained was also distinctive. My entire family referred to this kind of umbrella as a "Chamberlain," and I was of course the only person in the family to have one. "Chamberlain" came from the name of the British prime minister of the late 1930s, Neville Chamberlain, who was never seen without this particular wardrobe item. It became a brand name, and then a common name. My umbrella rapidly became a topic of conversation in the whole family: I was decidedly bizarre, eccentric. I was always looking out the window to see if it was going to rain the next day, and my mother, who saw what I was up to, made fun of me: "Checking the weather to figure out if you can go be all fancy with your brolly?" She rarely used the word "umbrella" [*parapluie*]; she almost always said "brolly" [*pébroc*].

• I had asked my mother to buy me a small record player. Using coupons you could cut out of the supplements from the local newspaper, I was able to order records of classical music reasonably cheaply. I had decided it was something I wanted to know about: a Tchaikovsky symphony, Ravel's Boléro, Bartók's *Concerto for Orchestra*… My taste was hesitant. I had no real reference points. I was dependent on what the newspaper put on offer.

When my mother would talk about me: "He listens to serious music now. It's like being at church."

• Every evening, when she got home from the factory, my mother would sit down in an armchair and take a fifteen-minute nap. She reminded me of this when we were talking about these years: "Never any longer than that," she insisted. "That was all I needed to recuperate. After that I was good."

And then her second workday would begin: shopping, cooking, washing up…

• She would iron the whole family's laundry standing up in the dining room, listening on a transistor radio (and later on a compact stereo system) to a radio station that mainly broadcast game shows or variety shows, and where advertisements took up huge chunks of airtime. She never turned the radio off, and this background noise never seemed to bother her, whereas I found it unbearable. She was probably barely listening to it.

• One day, my mother bought a knitting machine. It looked like an ironing board with a kind of metal grill on the top and a shuttle that passed back and forth in both directions. She would sit for hours in front of this bizarre device, which made a huge amount of noise. She made sweaters, cardigans, and scarves, following patterns that she cut out of the newspaper. The results were not always successful, because the machine was not very flexible and churned out knit panels that she would then have to join together. But it was faster than knitting by hand with needles, especially since her work at the factory had already damaged her finger joints, making this kind of work (which she had accomplished easily in the past) much more difficult for her.

• One day while I was still living with my parents, I was watching a television interview with Simone de Beauvoir on the condition of women, and my mother stopped to watch with me for a few minutes before remarking: "It's true what she's saying. She's right." Then she went back to her housework. She would never have gone so far as to read *The Second Sex,* of course. She had never even heard about it. Nor would she ever have called herself a feminist. But this is a good passing example of the importance television programs can have—profiles, interviews, documentaries...—even if it has to be added that she would not have seen or heard any of this particular program if I hadn't been watching it at that particular moment.

• My mother always enjoyed watching television series and also televised films. She preferred French films. She would only watch foreign films if they were dubbed into French. She couldn't watch a film in its original version with subtitles. When she saw one of those, she would stop and change the channel right away, muttering: "It's not in French." She never went to see films in a movie theater, at least not once she was married. I think she would go with her sister from time to time when she was younger, because she told me how, one night when they were leaving the theater after seeing a horror movie, they were so frightened they ran all the way home. She liked crime movies the best. And she loved

Alain Delon. "My Alain," she would say over and over again, when one of his films was on the schedule for the evening. "He's so handsome, my Alain. I love him." It would drive my father crazy with rage, which was doubtless what she was aiming for.

• Much later now, this time after the death of my father, when I had started visiting her again, a very ordinary conversation brought the cultural distance between us (which never fully disappeared, of course, but sometimes faded into the background) sharply back into place. We were having coffee at the kitchen table in her little house in Muizon. She was staring out the window, and I couldn't figure out what it was that had so caught her attention.

"What are you staring at like that?"

"The trees. The leaves that are falling. It's a strange thing."

I responded thoughtlessly: "It's called seasons."

She sat up straight: "Oh really? You know, I can spend time thinking too."

She wanted to show me that she wasn't "stupid," as she repeated two or three times, and that she thought about metaphysical kinds of questions (even if she didn't know that word).

In point of fact, in this case she was right: It is a strange thing, when you think about it, the falling leaves. Seasons are a strange thing... And these are questions that have no end. Kant, who underscored the limits of human understanding, knew this as well as anyone: there is no point in getting caught up in big, ultimate kinds of questions, to which no answer can ever be found. But that doesn't mean one cannot sometimes meditate on such things. I would have done better to join in with my mother's thinking and say to her: "Yes, you're right." Agreeing with her in that way would, I think, have made her happy.

• Each year, on the feast day of Saint Didier in May, or on my birthday in July, she would send me a check, so that I could buy myself something I would enjoy. I would cash the check so she wouldn't be hurt. It would always be a check for twenty euros. I imagine she sent the same thing to my brothers and to their children, on the same occasions. For her, when you think about it, it must have been a significant amount of money. I was always quite touched, but it also made me uncomfortable. We really lived on different planets if she thought that I would be able to buy myself something for twenty euros. Of course, it is the thought that counts… But she needed the money more than I did. For me, in the end, it was the price of a book. And so I would go buy one so that I could say to her: "Thank you! I bought myself a book I've been wanting to read for a long time."

• She never went to the theater or to concerts. And yet at the end of her life she would become a character in a play. Thomas Ostermeier, when he was making an adaptation of *Returning to Reims*, wanted to film a scene that would correspond to the opening of my book, when I am looking through photographs with her. At first I said no. I didn't have any desire for people to see and hear my mother on big screens in theaters across Europe. He persisted, and confided in me: "You know, I felt ashamed of my mother too. I would never invite her to my premieres, because I was afraid someone would ask me: 'Who is that strange lady over there?'"

And Geoffroy said to me: "You call yourself a radical, but you don't want anyone to see your mother in a film because you would feel ashamed of her???"

He was right. So in the end I accepted.

In fact, I was convinced that she would refuse, because, to put it mildly, she had not liked my book. But when I asked her, far from refusing, she exclaimed: "Yes! I would love to do that!" And she added with a laugh: "Oh my, oh my, at my age I'm going to be in a movie!"

Thomas Ostermeier came with his team, and they spent over an hour filming us. Before they left, Thomas, who is kindness itself, said to my mother: "We will come get you and bring you to the premier in Berlin, ma'am." She asked me several times in the next few months: "He is still planning to come get me, your friend?" I replied: "Yes, of course… Maybe not himself personally, but he will send someone to help you with the trip. And he will be there at the theater to welcome you." The first time we had this conversation, I added what I thought was a small and necessary warning, so that she wouldn't get off the plane and suddenly say "I want to go back home. I don't want to be here!": "Remember that it will be in Berlin. It might be a bit difficult for you, since you hate Germans so much…" But she brushed this objection aside: "Oh no! It wasn't their fault… Your friends weren't even born yet."

Alas, at the moment the production happened, she was in her bed in the nursing home unable to move. She never saw herself "in a movie" (in reality, in a few moments of a film that was part of a play). But I still have the images of her filmed that day. I'm chatting with her, and we are laughing.

• She often said to me: "The one trip I'd really like to take is to America. I've always dreamed of going to New York."

But she never did.

• In his book, *La matière de l'absence* (*The Matter of Absence*), Patrick Chamoiseau writes the following lines about his mother, ones that could also apply to mine:

> Up before dawn so many times, so many loads of wash, so much shopping, so much cooking, so many strategies for living, for surviving, so much shame gone through and so much fleeting pride, so many failures and so much success... *but never celebrated in a day's tumult!* And who remembers now?[87]

• I am fully aware today that it is both in opposition to her and thanks to her that I became who I am. In my mind the "in opposition to her" was for a long time stronger than the "thanks to her." I have been ashamed, obviously, and for a long time now, of the selfishness and the ingratitude I displayed. It pains me to think of the pain that selfishness and ingratitude caused her. But, as Albert Cohen would have said in his *Book of My Mother*, it is "a bit late in the day" for this bad conscience of mine.

IV

1

As I was leaving my mother on the day after she moved into the nursing home, I said to myself that there were two books I already knew well that now I needed to read again. I had the intuition that they would help me understand what was going on. The books were Simone de Beauvoir's *Old Age* and Norbert Elias's *The Loneliness of the Dying*. Everything happened so quickly that it was only after her death that I reread them.

When the French translation of Elias's book appeared, in 1987, I had been fascinated by the beauty of this text. I went to meet him so that I could write a profile of him (as they say in the world of journalism) for a French weekly magazine that I was writing for at the time. Elias lived in Amsterdam. This was not the first time I had met him. I had admired him for a long time and as a young journalist, as I was just getting started in the profession, I went to Bielefeld, in northern Germany, where he was a "researcher in residence," to interview him for a different newspaper. His university career had had many ups and downs. He had always been a marginal figure. As we know, universities are hardly welcoming to innovative and independent thinkers: they celebrate them in retrospect, forgetting that they resisted offering them any recognition while they were alive. In Amsterdam, he lived in the upstairs flat of a house, and his apartment was filled with small African statues that he had brought back from Ghana, where he had taught for many years. He was ninety years old, but he arranged to meet me at ten at night. When he had said in English on the telephone, "Tomorrow at ten," I had asked, "ten a.m.?" He answered, "No, no, ten p.m." We spoke for a long time, far into the night. We spoke about his book, of course, about his life and his work, and also about Bourdieu, who was one of the rare contemporary writers whose work he found interesting, and with whom he kept up a professional correspondence. I was on familiar ground.

Back then I did not know—or else I had forgotten—that Michel Foucault had wanted to translate this book, which was published in German in 1982. It's not surprising. He took an interest in Elias's work, of course, because it was while he was in the process of writing *Discipline and Punish* that Elias's *The Civilizing Process* was finally published (with quite a delay) in a French translation. He was drawn to the historical descriptions of the process of interiorization of mechanisms of social control and the installation of the "discipline" that a given culture demands at a certain moment.[88]

Clearly, Foucault's approach, in which he distinguished successive models for the functioning of power, was very different from that of Elias, who describes an evolutionary process over a long time period. But like Elias, Foucault was interested in sociohistoric transformations and their incorporation by individuals in the form of inculcated and interiorized behaviors. For Elias, social structures inscribe themselves in bodies; for Foucault, power circulates via bodies, it passes through them and shapes them. In both cases it is possible to speak of "disciplined" bodies, even if discipline's mechanisms are not the same for each of them. Is it possible that Foucault was later drawn to the book on old age and death by way of a kind of echo effect or a muted premonition of what he was in the process of living through, just as, in the same moment, his research into the "care of the self" in ancient culture can be read as a journal of his own quest for philosophical serenity in the face of illness and the approach of death?

In any case, I didn't know of—or didn't remember—the interest that Foucault had taken in *The Loneliness of the Dying* when I chose for an epigraph for the first (1989) edition of my biography of him a phrase from Elias's book: "Death conceals no mystery. It opens no door. It is the end of a human being. He is survived by the things he has given other human beings, by the things remaining in their memory."[89]

It is also worth citing here the sentence that comes just before: "Perhaps we ought to speak more openly and clearly about death, even if it is by ceasing to present it as a mystery."

While it does contain some beautiful pages about death, the book might just as well have been called *Growing Old* or *On Aging*. For, as Elias remarks, if science has studied in detail "physiological processes" and their medical consequences, there are fewer works that take up "the experience of ageing itself."[90] But doing so would be necessary for anyone wanting to understand how this experience changes the behaviors, the ways of being, and the psyches of those going through it.

Indeed, Elias emphasizes that it is necessary to have experienced the effects of aging oneself, the diminishing of physical and mental capacities, in order to truly understand all that is transformed in one's relation to the world, to others, to social life, to social norms, and so on. He takes the example of an older man who provokes laughter when he has trouble getting up out of a chair that is too low for him and in which someone foolishly invited him to sit. He insists on how "the experience of ageing people cannot be understood *unless we realize that the process of ageing often brings about a fundamental change in a person's position in society, and so in his or her whole relationship to other people.*" He emphasizes that "now that I myself am old I know, as it were, from the other side how difficult it is for people, young or middle-aged, to understand the situation and the experience of old people." This lack of "empathy" for older people, along with the inability of younger and healthier people "to imagine" the situation and the feelings of those whose strength is lessening, whose capacity for independent movement is diminishing, can be found any and everywhere. Who could disagree with Elias when he writes that "it is not easy to imagine that one's own body, which is so fresh and often so full of pleasant feelings, could become sluggish, tired and clumsy. … To put it differently, identification with the ageing and dying understandably poses special difficulties for people of other age groups. Whether consciously or unconsciously, people resist the idea of their own ageing and dying as best they can."[91]

Note that even though Elias presents himself here as an older person, who is now on "the other side," he continues to speak almost all the time from the point of view of younger, healthy people, all the time emphasizing that it is because he is no longer one of them that he can—that he must—ask the questions he asks. He underscores the need to change the direction of one's gaze, and to take as a point of departure for one's analysis the attitude toward the world of those whose physical autonomy and mobility have been reduced or have atrophied.

Analogous remarks can be found in Simone de Beauvoir's writing: "In earlier days I never paid much attention to older people; I looked upon them as the dead whose legs still kept moving. Now I see them—men and women only a little older than myself," she writes in a short story from 1967, "The Age of Discretion."[92] In this highly autobiographical text, she describes her reactions when she notices the persistent presence in herself of the signs that old age is arriving or the presentiment that it is about to arrive.

This turns out to be the moment at which she sets out to write the monumental work that she publishes in 1970, *Old Age*. Why does she decide to write this book? It is because, as she says in her memoirs, "I feel the need to understand the condition that is mine in a general way. Being a woman, I wished to throw light upon the condition of women; approaching old age, I wished to know how the conditions of old people are defined."[93]

The biographical roots of an intellectual project are here explicitly acknowledged. Both Elias's book and Beauvoir's originate in a moment where something in their life has shifted or is about to shift. Their entire way of looking at the world around them changes. They see both people and things differently because their experience of them is different.

Still, I want to expand the relevance of the remarks that I've just cited: They do not just apply to the slower, more limited or impeded gestures made by the older people that you now notice around you in daily life because you begin to feel some proximity to them, or perhaps because of the sharpened awareness you have of their weakness, of the physical and cognitive deficits that they experience. They apply more generally as well to the social and cultural perception of old age, as both Elias and Beauvoir make clear. They apply to what we think and to what we write: it is almost always older authors, or those who are starting to feel themselves become "old," who set themselves to thinking and writing about aging, about being older, about extreme old age. They are the ones who feel drawn to do this or called to it. The exception, of course, would be novels or autobiographies in which we see old age incarnated in the portraits of parents, or relations, or of key figures in the story being told. Many literary texts are devoted, entirely or in part, to the old age or the death of a parent or relative. Examples are not hard to come by, and I've cited a few over the course of the preceding chapters. (Beauvoir explores this territory across multiple centuries in *Old Age*.)

This is an area in which literature not only sees and shows a good deal more than theory does. It also thinks better and more deeply than does philosophy (taken in a wide sense). Theory is generally written by people who are in full possession of their physical and mental faculties, and who are therefore, in this regard, on the side of the "dominants," the "privileged," because they are on the near side of the barrier that Elias evokes—whatever may be the modalities of their inferiorization or their vulnerability in other respects (economic, social, political, cultural, or based on gender, sex, or race...), and whatever their critical engagements might be in these arenas.

It is the case that the question of old age allows us to interrogate certain philosophical conceptions and political theories on the question of what remains outside their field of vision. More fundamentally still, we could ask about what they are required to ignore as they establish the scope of their concepts. The exclusion of certain realities seems often to be an inevitable and intrinsic condition for the definition of concepts and for their mobilization and use. To think about one problem is necessarily not to think about others. In this instance it is as if extreme old age somehow fails to be included in the conceptual register, as if most concepts from philosophy or political theory cannot or will not see old age and old people. In many ways, old age not only finds itself socially relegated; it is also occulted conceptually. Tacitly sidelined, at the best, to the fields of perception and affect, it holds barely any place in the philosophical sphere; it rarely finds itself envisioned in any theoretical elaboration.

Let's take an example that will show that I am myself implicated in the critique I am elaborating here. In *Returning to Reims*, I cited a famous phrase from Sartre's *Saint Genet*, one that had struck me deeply when I was a student. It felt so illuminating that I took it, a bit naively, as a motto for my life: "What is important is not what people make of us but what we ourselves make of what they have made of us." What a magnificent sentence! An uplifting one. It comes to us cloaked in an aura of emancipatory power, despite all the obvious limitations—social, cultural, racial, or related to sex and gender—that are there in the heart of the way it is formulated and that it carries with it at the very moment that it calls to us to move beyond such limitations, to evade them. I see this now, but acted as if I didn't in the past.

In any case, one thing is very clear: we can only take this sentence to heart, as a motto for our existence, if there is time in front of us. Any one of us would need to have an open future, in the course of whose realization it may be possible, to some degree, to act upon what social and historical structures have done to us, in order to transform ourselves, to choose what we are going to become, to reinvent ourselves. For that sentence to be meaningful, we must have our life in front of us. I wasn't even twenty years old when those words inspired me! We would, at the very least, need to have some life in front of us. I am tempted to say that this was the case for my mother when, at the age of eighty, she began a new love story, shaking off all that the social structures and constraints around her had done to her in order to construct a new present and a new future for herself. Yet what about someone still older than her, or someone no longer independent, or, a fortiori, someone who can no longer leave their room, or get out of bed, in a geriatric hospital or a nursing home (as would be the case for my mother at eighty-seven)? In that case the Sartrean statement no longer has any meaning. That is a situation in which nothing can be changed regarding what has been done to us, and even one in which it is no longer possible to change what is happening on a daily basis. Time is frozen. There is no longer any possibility to project yourself into the future, not even into the most immediate future. This does not invalidate the meaning of Sartre's sentence, nor its beauty. But it does severely limit the scope of its applicability: it excludes people who are in extreme old age and dependent.

Consider as well some central Sartrian concepts, like "freedom" in *Being and Nothingness* (1943), or "fused-group" or "pledge" in *Critique of Dialectical Reason* (1960). They can only apply to those who have the physical and mental capacity to establish themselves as "project" or as "nihilation" (to separate yourself from what is, to "nihilate" it by projecting yourself into some future) in the first book, or, in the second one, which is in dialogue with Marxist thought, to join a *praxis* in which you are fully engaged in a mobilized collective, one conscious of itself as a collective in action and affirming of its own self-determination.

In Sartre's vocabulary, "being" is "immanence," "facticity," "in-itself" (or later, it is the "practico-inert"); "nothingness" is "transcendence," "freedom," "for-itself" (or later, it is "praxis" and the "group-in-fusion").

In each of these two moments of Sartre's thought, it is the same idea that constitutes the central point of the philosophical system: the point at which you tear yourself away from the past and the present, from "being" or the "practico-inert," in order to define yourself as moving beyond yourself, as an existence still to come. In both cases, the concepts are necessarily tied to those of temporality. The principial presupposition here, and one moreover thematized as such, is a relationship of consciousness—either individual or collective—to an open temporality, to the possibility of a "project," be it an individual or a collective one.

To run away from freedom, to run away from *one's own* freedom, is to fall into inauthenticity and "bad faith." But what possibility of something yet to come is left for someone in a nursing home, for someone no longer able to get out of bed? Older people in a state of dependence are not running away from their freedom: they no longer have any. They have no choice. Old age has no place in this philosophy.

It is quite remarkable how the situation is exactly the same in Beauvoir's work before she begins writing about the "elderly" (*les vieillards*—her word). Look at the introduction to *The Second Sex*, and you will see that the work unfolds within a theoretical framework that has almost no relevance to the people in whom she will take an interest only much later, in *Old Age*. Here is an example:

> The perspective we have adopted is one of existentialist morality. Every subject posits itself as a transcendence concretely, through projects; it accomplishes its freedom only by perpetual surpassing towards other freedoms; there is no other justification for present existence than its expansion towards an indefinitely open future.

It is not necessary to spend much time thinking about these sentences or the one that follows to see that Beauvoir is not yet thinking about older people:

> Every time transcendence lapses into immanence, there is a degradation of existence into "in-itself," of freedom into facticity; this fall is a moral fault if the subject consents to it; if this fall is inflicted on the subject, it takes the form of frustration and oppression; in both cases it is an absolute evil.[94]

The idea of a "moral fault" that Beauvoir employs here to describe the situation of women who "consent" to their "condition" seems quite strange in the introduction to a book wholly devoted to exploring the history and the present moment of the inferiorization of women. One might have expected that she would take up the way in which the structures of the social and sexual orders are incorporated by individuals.

Sartrean subjectivism, carried to an extreme, becomes here intellectual moralism. When she takes up the question of old age, she will have to rework her categories of thought in a profound way.

For older people, in fact, it is not that transcendence falls away, that the "for itself" degrades into an "in itself." Rather, there is no longer an "open future" nor any possibility of an "open future": there is no longer any transcendence or any possibility of it; the "for itself" is inexorably undermined, corroded by the "in itself," which settles in more and more definitively.

Much the same thing can be said about Merleau-Ponty, when he defines the human subject, in his *Phenomenology of Perception*, as the experience each person has of their body as they explore the sensory world, as the involvement of the body in space and time. If, as a consequence, human freedom unfolds as the affirmation of being-in-the-world as spatiality and temporality—as spatialization and temporalization—this necessarily involves an exclusion, an implicit one perhaps, of those who are situated outside of the space and time of "normal" people, "normal" people being here young ones, those in good health, capable of moving around in space with ease and of projecting themselves forward in time… All of the chapters of Merleau-Ponty's treatise deal with—only deal with—the world of autonomous, able-bodied, mobile people.[95]

The way old age is obscured within phenomenological and existentialist philosophy is flagrantly obvious in the works I have just cited. Let us consider philosophy more generally, by extending the invitation that Elias offered us regarding attitudes from daily life: to reexamine them from the point of view of older people. Or what if we reexamine philosophical discourses on the basis of the critique that Beauvoir herself offers in her book from 1970? What will we learn about the scope or pertinence of most of the fundamental concepts of philosophy by bringing up the question of old age? I am thinking of political philosophy in particular, and concepts such as "social contract," "general will," "assembly of people," "public space," "deliberation," "rational discussion," "consensus," "dissensus," "the power to act," "emancipation," "public speech," "political action," "collective opinion," "political organizing," "street actions," "revolt," "civil disobedience," "resistance," and so on. It is quite difficult to find a place here for the various dimensions of—I mean the actual reality of—extreme old age, of physical incapacity, of disability, of cognitive decline. What is being set aside here is not a set of questions that theory has no need to bother with in order to apprehend this phenomenon or that; it is also not a question of a blind spot for thought, of the kind that can inevitably be found in any theoretical approach or any conceptual elaboration. No, what we have here runs deeper; it is something that seems to be an intrinsic, internal limit of a concept and of the theory that puts it to use; it is something that a theory or a concept is not able to include. To bring up old age is to make visible everything that most theories have had to leave in the shadows in order for their concepts to function, everything that cannot be or must not be taken into consideration so that a concept can occupy the place it has been given, the place that has been designed or designated for it. Yet a moment always comes for the return of the repressed, and at that point the need for a theoretical reconfiguration becomes obvious... If these existential realities are not, or cannot, be taken into consideration within such theories and concepts, then those theories and concepts themselves must become the object of a critical interrogation that comes from outside, one that is addressed to what such theories forget or exclude—what they have needed to forget and exclude in order to be elaborated in the first place. In this we can follow the path laid out by Beauvoir, whose 1970 volume can be read as a self-critique (a critique both of herself and of Sartre), and also as a critique of philosophy in general.

Any concept of the "body" that, setting out to think about daily life and one's presence to the world, or to think about political action, finds it necessary to leave aging, physical weakness, illness, and so on out of its field of perception will, in so doing, consign older people or people who have lost their autonomy to nearly total invisibility: they will have no place within that theory. They will be rendered absent by the theoretical gaze itself. Theories of the body as a political body, and of politics as the presence of the body in public space, push outside the frame they themselves construct for the emergence of politics as such all those who cannot, or who can no longer, "take to the streets," as the traditional expression has it.

I am perfectly aware that a concept is not a replication or a reflection of reality, but rather that which allows reality to be understood, to take on meaning. An abstract idea is not a replica of concrete reality; one might even claim that it is what allows for the construction of reality in such a way that it can be perceived and understood. A concept organizes dispersed empirical realities, ordering them in meaningful ways: thinking is classifying.

In order to distinguish clearly the specificity of the theoretical domain as opposed to the empirical, Louis Althusser liked to say, claiming (erroneously) that he was citing Spinoza, that "the concept of a dog does not bark." It's undeniable. Concepts don't bark! In fact, in his treatise *On the Improvement of the Understanding*, Spinoza distinguishes between a circle and the idea of a circle. The idea of a circle has no center and no circumference. He also distinguishes between a body and the idea of a body. The idea of a body is not the body itself: "A true idea (for we possess a true idea) is something different from its correlate (*ideatum*); thus a circle is different from the idea of a circle. The idea of a circle is not something having a circumference and a center, as a circle has; nor is the idea of a body that body itself."[96] It nonetheless goes without saying that any idea of a circle that would fail to include in its definition the center and the circumference would at the least be incomplete. And, thinking of Althusser's statement, how could one imagine a dog, even an ideal of one, a conceptual one, that would not bark? What would be the pertinence of a concept of a dog that did not contain barking or, at least, the possibility of barking? The same is true for the idea of a body that would not include age, aging, the loss of autonomy, and so on.

Philosophical concepts thus presuppose, in a fairly general way, what Elias's example suggests, that everybody is able to stand up without difficulty out of a chair that is too low. The body can, of course, be tired, fragile, vulnerable, ill; it could be a minority body, in a state of precarity, inferiorized… Nonetheless, for political theory it remains a body that is standing, or that in any case can stand, can move, can act.

I don't wish to be misunderstood. To insist on a lack or an absence in theoretical projects need not—not necessarily—be taken as an accusation or an indictment, and certainly not as a condemnation of this or that body of thought or this or that set of theoretical principles. When someone sets out to develop a theoretical analysis, to develop concepts in order to deal with a particular question, they will inevitably set many other questions aside. It isn't possible to write about everything at the same time. We should admit that an absolute theory, just like the total book Mallarmé dreamed of, does not and cannot exist, even if Hegel or Sartre imagined themselves to have built one. Moreover, focusing on a particular reality has as an unavoidable condition and a necessary consequence that one will not be focusing on others, even neighboring ones. A concept is always partial, specific, limited, provisional, even if it is not presented as such, even if it lays claim to a certain generality or universality. We also know that there will always be questions that have yet to be constituted as such, and that slowly become pressing, or are made pressing, when they are brought forward by political and social movements or through intellectual interventions. (These two levels are linked to each other, since a movement is always accompanied by a body of theoretical reflections, and gives rise to an efflorescence of historical, sociological, cultural, and literary studies.) In such a case, people come to reinterrogate not only history—"my quarrel with history," Édouard Glissant said in *Caribbean Discourse*, when calling into question historical accounts that present themselves as universal, but in which he found no place for himself as someone belonging to a colonized world—but also the theories and concepts in use and, along with them, the entire culture that underlies and supports them.

2

All of this explains why I am tempted to associate the book that Beauvoir wrote about old age with the one Foucault wrote about madness. They are separated by barely ten years: *Histoire de la folie* (*History of Madness*)[97] was published in 1961; *La vieillesse* (*Old Age*—but which might just as well have been titled *Histoire de la vieillesse,* or *A History of Old Age*) in 1970. We can consider them to be contemporaries of each other. And despite all their differences—notably in the fields they are thinking about and intervening in, still, in their theoretical frameworks (existentialist philosophy for Beauvoir, a structuralist method for Foucault), in the historical periodizations involved, in their references, in their writing style, and so on—they resemble each other in astonishing ways. In both cases, we find an exploration of multiple cultural strata in order to see where and how divisions are put into place, how boundaries are established, how exclusions and relegations work.

We could take them as two archaeologies of culture that have been consigned to two enormous volumes. Foucault took six hundred pages to work through his project of excavation; Beauvoir took nearly seven hundred. Foucault wanted to write an "archaeology of [a] silence" and it is striking that Beauvoir should make use of similar language about old age. She declares in her introduction: "The very reason why I am writing this book [is] to break the conspiracy of silence."[98]

Two "archaeologies" of culture, then, but also two "histories of the present," because in both instances it is a question of understanding the world we live in today by starting from a study that we might call both "ethnological" (writing the ethnology of your own culture, exploring what is familiar ground by digging through the various successive strata that constitute it) and "genealogical" (rediscovering and analyzing the "birth" of the institutions that have become so "natural" within our social landscape that we no longer question them).[99]

In *History of Madness*, Foucault deciphers, in the philosophical project that Descartes lays out as he sets up the Cogito ("I think"), one of the emblematic gestures in the great division between reason and unreason that is put in place during the seventeenth century at all levels of social and cultural life. At the very beginning of *Meditations on First Philosophy*, as he is wondering what discourses might cast doubt upon the certainties and the truths that a consciousness finds within itself, Descartes in fact mentions "madmen, whose brains are so damaged … that they firmly maintain they are kings when they are paupers." But he sets aside this objection with an exclamation: "But such people are insane."[100] Foucault uncovers in this passage one of the paradigmatic gestures by which madness is excluded, and he makes a connection between this philosophical exclusion and the establishment, at this same time, of the general hospital, in which a large, heterogeneous population will be forcibly interned. It is not only the "insane" who are locked up, but also "the venereal, the debauched, the dissolute, blasphemers, homosexuals, alchemists and libertines," and also "prostitutes," along with "the poor and disabled, the elderly poor, beggars, the work-shy … in short, all those who, in relation to the order of reason, morality, and society, showed signs of 'derangement.'"[101] So for Foucault in his history of madness, it was a question of making apparent the "principle of coherence" that links together a metaphysical text and a politico-administrative act. These two elements, these two events, or, better, these two "aspects" of a single event, express, or together serve to translate, but in different spheres, "in both the order of speculation and the order of institutions, in both discourse and decree," the establishment of a new "moral sensibility." It happens on every level, "in all the places where a significant element can take on for us the value of language."[102]

Would it be possible, by transposing Foucault's analysis to the questions at play in the book I am writing here, to put forward the idea that a good part of the Western philosophical tradition was constituted, and continues to constitute itself, via the institution and reiteration of an analogous gesture of exclusion? "But these are old people" is something so many philosophical works seem to repeat secretly, surreptitiously. They are works in which a line of demarcation would no longer separate reason and unreason, but rather youth and old age, good health and physical incapacity, independence and dependence of movement. This exclusion of old age from the order of discourse and from theory might be described, using a single principle of structural analogy, or rather of structural isomorphism, as an aspect of a wider cultural configuration of which the institutionalization of older people would be another aspect.

Of course, this rejection of old age is not directly stated in the way Foucault tells us is the case for Descartes confronting madness. More often than not it is tacit, implicit, and it mostly passes unnoticed both by those formulating it and by those reading it. But this does not mean that, once you begin to raise this question and to look more closely, this rejection is not just as obvious, just as clear, just as enormous, and just as effective as that applied to "unreason" according to Foucault's analysis. Basically, everything happens as if certain philosophical systems had set limits to the applicability of their fundamental concepts and ignored or dismissed the world of old age, of extreme old age, of those who have lost their physical autonomy… Entire conceptual architectures are built up on this exclusion, even when it is not explicitly thematized. One cannot turn to something like a "collective unconscious" to explain this. The process of relegation is anchored in what Foucault would have called "the thick historical layers of an *experiment*."[103] Basically, what we see in play here is, to use another of Foucault's expressions, "the relationship of a culture to the very thing that it excludes," to its outside.[104]

What seems particularly important to me in the approach proposed by Foucault, when he undertakes this archaeology of culture, is his insistence on the fact that what he is doing is not elaborating an analysis of concepts. His intention is rather to reinscribe concepts and that which presents itself in the form of scientific developments (in this particular case, psychiatry, psychology, psychoanalysis) within the historical structures that govern different forms of the experiment in which the exclusion of madness is at stake. Psychiatry only became possible once this relegation had been accomplished. The concepts are joined together with the relegation that makes them possible.

So it will be in literature and the arts that Foucault will find the suppressed voice of madness: Goya, Van Gogh, Artaud… A special place is given over to the work of Nietzsche. Foucault brought in the figure of Nietzsche as a means of invoking the "possibility of the mad philosopher," a possibility excluded from the rationalist tradition. Beauvoir also draws on art and literature because she wants voices that have been reduced to silence nonetheless to be heard. She wishes not only to study the ways in which old age is and has been viewed, both yesterday and today; her book is also a gesture that makes an autobiographical claim. It affirms the possibility of an old philosopher, and specifically of an old philosopher (or one who is about to be old) who is also a woman, someone who experiences the world differently and who integrates into her thought the particular and crucial dimension of aging, her own aging, and the interest that process produces in her for other people who have preceded her on this path. She not only writes about age, on the subject of old age; she writes from the point of view of old age, an old age that is just beginning or that is about to arrive. This is what Norbert Elias also did, in a book a good deal shorter, of course, but which nonetheless reads as if it were a reply to Beauvoir's challenge. It is also what Jean Améry seems to have done when, in a state between "revolt and resignation," he took up the question of aging, of his own process of aging.[105]

If philosophy and political theory participate in the exclusion of old age, in the relegation of old people, by the way they elaborate concepts that leave no place for such people, no space for them, and, even more fundamentally, by elaborating concepts that lack the capacity to grant them any space or any place, then we need now to ask a series of fundamental questions that might be summed up in two principial statements, with the aim of reintegrating these absences into the field of thought and also into the field of action. First, any social theory, any political theory that wishes to think of itself as critical and as emancipatory needs to ask itself: Can old people speak? Then, if that is not the case: What can be done, what needs to be done, so that they can be heard even if they do not speak?

3

Beauvoir confides in her memoirs, when she is describing the genesis of her work on *Old Age*, that she wanted to write an essay that would be "the counterpart of *The Second Sex*, but dealing with old people."[106] It is easy to see the symmetry between the two works. The approach is similar: describe and analyze the situation of a category of inferiorized people, people assigned to a subaltern position, "secondary" in the social world. There is, however, a notable difference between the two projects, in the way she describes each of them at the outset. In the opening pages of *The Second Sex*, in 1949, she poses the question, in effect, of why women do not say "we," as do working-class people or Blacks in the United States. (These are her examples.) In answer to her own question, she insists on how political and social movements are anchored geographically and spatially: it is the fact of sharing the same neighborhoods, the same workplaces, and so on, that allows for the formation of a collective subject, of a first-person-plural form of speech. For women "as women," on the other hand, the situation is more complicated because, she says, "they live dispersed among men." She also insists, and this is essential, that a working-class woman would feel more solidarity with her working-class husband than with bourgeois women, or that a Black woman would feel more solidarity with her Black husband than with white women (with something similar also being the case, of course, for bourgeois women and white women). How then, could a "we" be constructed when there is so much to hold apart the persons who would be likely to form it, to give life to any such "we"?[107] This is obviously a major problem regarding the way the social world is divided up into different categories and the way different possible "we's" are juxtaposed or even in competition or in actual conflict with each other. A "we" that comes into existence must first of all affirm itself by breaking from, or even by opposing itself to, the other "wes" that already exist. It must impose the principle behind its point of view, the principle behind its categorization, the principle that founds its existence and its legitimacy.

Consequently, Beauvoir's entire book is animated by this question: How can women, confined to a "subordinate" status, and at the moment she is writing the objects of the gaze and the discourse of men (whatever their position in the social world may be), contest their status and become subjects of their own gaze and their own discourse?

Having arrived at the end of her investigation, which takes up two volumes and more than one thousand pages, Beauvoir does not really offer an answer to the question she asks at the outset, but she does describe in almost lyrical terms the appearance of a horizon of freedom (even if the perspectives she describes seem to have more to do with individual as opposed to collective forms of freedom). We are moving, there can be no doubt, "toward liberation," as the title of the final part of the book announces. That final part contains only one chapter before arriving at the conclusion, and it bears the title "The Independent Woman."

Obviously things do not proceed in the same manner when her interest is in old people. About the "elderly," she writes: "I wanted to describe truthfully the condition of these parias and the ways in which they experience that condition." But that is where the symmetry ends. She does not ask why those she calls the "elderly" do not say "we." She does not ask how people in extreme old age, diminished and dependent, could become the subjects of their own speech, of their own gaze, of their own lives. The reason for this is simple: she knows that they cannot do so. That is, in fact, what is at the heart of her book. How could these people who have become weak, who are often experiencing varying degrees of a loss of autonomy, who are sometimes experiencing cognitive decline constitute a "we," become the collective subject of a discourse spoken in the first-person plural? To transition from the state of "seriality" (a set of juxtaposed individuals, each one next to the other, but all of them separate) to that of a "group" (individuals united and mobilized collectively) is impossible for them—not only physically and mentally, but also materially. That is why she states with such determination that "I want to make their voices heard."[108]

By pointing out that Beauvoir does not ask the same question here as in the earlier work, and that she does not stop to think about this fundamental difference, of course I am not offering a reproach of any kind. *Old Age* was a major intervention into the intellectual and political field of a moment when these problems had barely been formulated or found to be worthy of interest. She invented new forms of questioning, and her innovative audacity should only be admired. But I do want to engage with her book around this question, because it connects to a whole series of issues having to do with social movements and political activism. There are also issues of political representation in play: if it is necessary for someone to arrange for the voices of old people to be heard, it is because those people's voices cannot be heard on their own. What kind of a group is it that cannot speak for itself, and that, consequently, would not speak if someone did not speak for it and, in speaking for it, thereby constitute it as a group that has things to say? The problem is equally perplexing if you look at it from the point of view of a spokesperson. What does it mean to speak for a group of individuals who would not speak if they were not spoken for—which is to say not only on their behalf but also in their place? What is the nature of this spokesperson function, which shows itself so clearly in this particular case?

My mother had been a political subject, when she was working and would follow her union's instructions, when she took part in strikes or slowdowns; when she voted for candidates on the left in elections, or when she decided to abstain. She was still a political subject, of course, when she began voting for the Right, for the extreme right. In each of these configurations, she participated in a collective opinion, she became part of a collective action. She always said "we." Even if the content and the meaning of this "we" might change as the years passed, she always spoke in the first-person plural. (She also said *on*, which in French can replace *nous* in day-to-day conversation. "Tomorrow, no one is going to vote. *On en a marre*. Everyone is—we are all—fed up.") To be a political subject meant being a part of something, in multiple ways and referring to different things: a part of some collective political subject. This collective subject, on which her personal judgment and her words both relied, was most often tied to a political party or some kind of a union organization. There was no spontaneously formed "we." It didn't just come from nowhere. When she lost her physical independence and then was admitted to a nursing home, the possibility of saying "we" disappeared. That brought her back to a place of inertia, the inertia of a serial set of people, unable to join together and deliberate, to speak out or, even less, to act.

Alone in her bed in the nursing home my mother did indeed protest; she proclaimed her indignation. But her cries were addressed to a single person: me. (Or perhaps to four people, if I count my brothers, whom she also telephoned.) It would usually happen in the evening or at night, and her anger had my answering machine for its only listener—to which I would then listen several hours later. She would say things that unquestionably had an eminently political dimension, there is no doubt about that. All you had to do was to listen to what she was saying not as her individual complaints, but rather to give back to her words their general applicability, to hear them precisely as the denunciation of an institution, of a system, and of their effects on the lives of people like her. But what kind of a political statement is it that remains shut up in the private sphere, that has no access to the public sphere? The conclusion is a simple one: my mother wept, but she had no access to speech, or at least to public speech. Her complaint never left her room.

It is certainly the case that in all the nursing homes taken together, there are thousands of older people who do the same thing: telephone their children or people close to them and give voice to their distress, to their unhappiness. But how are these older people, especially once they've lost their physical abilities, and sometimes some of their mental faculties, to join together, to think of themselves as a group with a political agenda, to affirm themselves as a "we," even if it were to be done by way of delegation to something like a union or a party? There is no audible "we" from people at an advanced age, because there is no real "we" that is possible, which means there is no public speech that is possible or imaginable.

Movements of retirees have, of course, existed for quite some time. This has obviously come about through the creation of special branches of unions that represent workers and continue to defend them once they are no longer working. Or it happens through the creation of organizations that develop their own platforms and agendas. In both cases, political actions take traditional forms: meetings, petitions, demonstrations, forms of pressure on public sources of power, and also conferences, newspaper and journal publications, studies of various kinds, and so on.[109]

But what about older people who are weak and dependent? Those who have lost their autonomy, who are isolated in nursing homes, and for whom it is hardly possible to take part in some kind of collective mobilization, to belong to an organization, or simply to become the public enunciators of some form of critical discourse? It is incumbent on others to become their spokespersons. Books describing the situation of older people in nursing homes are published by caregivers and by journalists. They inform us, reveal things to us, alarm us… We owe them thanks. But it is not the people concerned who write these books. No one can change this state of affairs. Thus we only know the reality experienced by these vulnerable and dependent individuals from an "exterior" point of view, and never from an "interior" one.

The "elderly" are therefore doomed forever to be a kind of category-object whose identity, whose image, and whose representation come from the exterior rather than the interior. Their status is always "granted" to them, Beauvoir says.[110] Perhaps they become a group of individuals relegated by the social world to a separate geographic space and a cultural and civic alterity. Perhaps they become a group someone sets up as such in order to defend their interests as a group, in which case, and this is the best-case scenario, they are given a political status as a "them," inevitably construed as passive: we stand beside them with empathy and speak for them. In speaking for them, none of the women or the men making up this "them" seems able to accede to the condition of a "we," the collective subject of a political discourse uttered in the first-person plural (nor to that of a first-person singular, it should also be added). The "we," if I can put it this way, comes to them from the outside. It is constituted by other people. The group exists because an exterior discourse constitutes it as a group.

It does seem to me, moreover, that Beauvoir limits and tends to dissolve the group whose voice she wishes to make heard when she states that the social, civic, and political destitution of which older people are the victims has to do with their lack of economic utility. "The aged do not form a body with any economic strength whatsoever and they have no possible way of enforcing their rights," she writes in her introduction. We can follow her up to that point. We can still follow her when she states that "society cares about the individual only insofar as they are profitable." Or when she emphasizes that "the age at which the decline into senility begins has always depended on the class to which one belongs." But we might not be so interested in following her when she adds, in a sentence that is obviously problematic in many ways, framed as it is by such a narrow economism, that "it is to the interest of the exploiting class to destroy the solidarity between the workers and the unproductive old so that there is no one at all to protect them."[111]

Do not these remarks undo the making of the group of the "elderly" at the very moment that Beauvoir is in the process of defining it as a practical ensemble, a group whose voice she intends to make heard? She reinscribes this specific category into an already established configuration: workers and the class that exploits them, a class struggle, and so on. The influence of Marxism on her thinking seems to win out over her intention to think through the existence of a defined category and to apprehend it as such. In a conversation with Sartre published in the final volume of his *Situations*, she criticizes the way he fails to admit the existence of a feminist movement except insofar as it fits into the general framework of the class struggle. She affirms and reaffirms the autonomy of this movement, which is organized around its own problems and its own specific demands.[112] Is there then not an identical kind of dilution into the global struggle that happens at the end of her book on old age, when she declares that it is not the "politics of old age" that needs to be improved? Rather, she says, it is "the whole system that is at issue," and "our claim cannot be otherwise than radical—change life itself."[113] Well, of course. Who could disagree with such a claim? But while we are waiting for this hypothetical general subversion, who is going to concern themselves with the concrete situation that the "elderly" are living in in nursing homes, the same older people to whose condition she devotes so many beautiful and moving pages?

The idea that there exists a plurality of possible principles for dividing things up, and that, unless you have a substantialist conception of the social world, none of them is more real, or more anchored in "reality," more important, than any other, leads to a fundamental political question: What are the conditions for the formation of what Sartre called a "practical ensemble," which is to say social groups that are politically mobilized? What I mean is: How do these groups constitute themselves? What are the modalities of this constitution? How are they formed against a background that is plural and multiple, always open to being divided up in new ways? What histories, what kinds of processes —both theoretical and practical—bring this about? How does what retrospectively appears as a potential principle for political categorization—sometimes quite an obvious one—become established as one of our modes of perception of the social world and of political struggle? I wrote in *Principes d'une pensée critique* (Principles for critical thought) that the group (in the Sartrean sense of a politically active collective) precedes—from a logical and political point of view, not a chronological one—seriality and makes seriality appear as such once the group has been established as a group. That is to say that political categorization produces the category as a modality for perceiving the social world, thereby giving it an existence in reality. Politics is an activity involving the performative production of the real. This is what Bourdieu in various texts from the 1980s so pertinently named the "theory effect." (To give a rapid and rough sketch of this: We are aware of social classes because Marx said that there were social classes, a working class, not just in the sense of a class in the concrete sense, in the objective reality of the workplace, but in the sense of an established category and a politically active group. As I showed in *Returning to Reims*, it is because there was a Communist Party that presented itself as the party of the working class and that spoke for the working class and in its name that that class existed both in discourse and in reality.)[114]

Every social movement has a tendency to impose the principle through which it divides up the world, one it aims to inscribe into reality as the principal social division: proletariat and bourgeoisie, women and men, homosexual and heterosexual, Blacks and whites, old and young, and so on. We know, for example, that Marxists or former ones who hold on to many aspects of Marxist thinking in their conception of the social world tend to declare that any struggles that are not directly part of the economic or class struggle are secondary or accessory ones. But there is a wider sense in which the idea that there is only one principal struggle haunts political thinking. We have seen how Beauvoir, so attentive to bringing to our attention specific forms of oppression, in taking up the struggle to support older people, nonetheless had a tendency to refer everything back to economics as the ground of everything. In a more general sense, every group that sets itself up as such or endeavors to do so tends to think that the way of dividing up the world that it uses to found its existence—class, race, gender, etc.—should be considered as the essential division, and therefore as the primary struggle. The concept of "intersectionality" provides, to a certain degree, if not a resolution to these contradictions, at least a way of taking them into account. But the plurality and the specificity of categorizations, of the principles for dividing up and perceiving the social world, of social movements themselves, seem to me not only insurmountable, but, more importantly, indispensable.

Finally, we need to come back to this question of the "spokesperson" that I raised earlier in relation to limit cases—that of my mother in her nursing home—and that I would like to generalize. Where there is a question that has been constituted as a political one, there are always spokespersons. This is because it is only when there are spokespersons, or on an even deeper level, it is because it is only through the speech of a spokesperson, that a question comes to be understood as a political one. This is particularly the case for dominated groups, and especially when they are economically or culturally dispossessed, or, in the case of older people, in physical or mental decline. This also means, of course, that the voice that the spokesperson makes heard is necessarily an interpreted or a reorganized one. Or it may indeed be entirely constructed and organized by the spokesperson, whatever their status (member of a union or a party or an organization, a writer or an intellectual...). A reflexive discourse, a theoretico-practical one, produces an analysis of the situation in question that is political, historical, and structural. It is that analysis that gives form and meaning to something that cannot be limited solely to the register of lived experience.

We find ourselves here at the limits of social mobilization and political activity. How indeed shall we think about the activity of those who can no longer act, about the speech of those who can no longer speak? Such is the case of those Beauvoir calls "old people." And yet this limit case allows us to question in a more general way both political categories and those of political theory. After all, there is no doubt that much the same could be said, but to different degrees, about the unemployed, about precarious workers, those who are only able to find temporary employment or part-time jobs or ones with no guarantees. (Being uncertain of employment weighs on people like a quiet threat, one that paralyzes feelings of rebellion and deprives people of any capacity for resistance.)

Is it enough, however, that someone speaks up for older people and brings their voice into the public arena so that their speech—an indirect version of it—can be heard and taken into account? So that it can have an impact? It may well not be. Consider this simple, eloquent fact: while *The Second Sex* is famous, has always been kept in print in paperback in France, and still figures almost continuously, even today, in the "Essays" section of the best-seller lists, while it is a classic on an international scale, read, cited, taught, commented on, discussed everywhere in the world, *Old Age* remains a book that is much less read and not very well known. This is something I've observed many times: whether it was at some public event or in a conversation with friends, any time I would say that the book I was working on could be thought of as in dialogue with this book of Beauvoir's, I realized not only that no one had ever read it, but that almost no one even knew that it existed, even among readers who knew her work quite well. This tells us that the intellectual elaboration of a problem, even by a writer as well known as Beauvoir, is not sufficient to impose that problem politically in a durable way and on a wide scale. For that to happen, the elaboration has to encounter some kind of social interest, a previously constituted social movement, even if it is in a latent state, or with a submerged or perhaps emerging existence: waiting for the elaboration. Moreover, the performative efficacy of a theoretical work when it comes to constituting a new mode of perception of the world and its divisions depends on the already partially established reality of the group as such, or on the possibility of the establishment of that group. But what if that group is not able to exist? If a movement of "old people" cannot exist, then a book devoted to them will not encounter the same kind of response that a work on women was able to find; it will not come to serve as a reference and a tool for succeeding generations to take up to help them think and act. Anyone involved in feminism today, or anyone who undertakes to think within the field of gender theory, will need to read what Simone de Beauvoir wrote in 1949. Of course, the work has been criticized. But if a work is still being criticized more than seventy years after it was published, it means that book is alive, that it exists in the present moment. But who today feels the need to read what Simone de Beauvoir was writing in 1970? Her treatise on old age? A thick volume devoted to "old people"? When you are young, these kinds of problems seem distant; as you grow older, you hardly feel drawn to read about this depressing subject; and then when you are old, you barely read any more, and if you do read, you prefer to read other things. Also, since there is no movement of the "elderly," of dependent older people, since there is no "we" to come into existence, a book whose intention is to substitute a "they" for this impossible "we" and to carry their speech into the public arena cannot hope to produce the same kind of effect that another book might produce, one with an immediate resonance with current social, cultural, and political activity.

This is, after all, the fundamental political question: Who speaks? Who is able to make themselves heard? And if this fundamental political gesture remains inaccessible to so many people who figure among the most dominated, the most dispossessed, the most vulnerable, does it not fall to writers, artists, and intellectuals to speak of them and for them, to make them visible and to "make their voices heard," to take up Simone de Beauvoir's expression again? Perhaps it is even necessary to "lend them a voice," the voice they do not have, the voice they no longer have—indeed, in the case of dependent older people, the voice they can never have again.

Notes

1. René Descartes, "Discourse on the Method," in *The Philosophical Writings of Descartes*, trans. John Cottingham, Robert Stoothoff, and Dugald Murdoch, vol. 1 (Cambridge University Press, 1985), 123–24.

2. Shichirô Fukazawa, *Étude à propos des chansons de Narayama*, trans. Bernard Frank (Gallimard, 1980). Frank insists, both in his preface to the first edition and in his afterword to the second edition, that this is not a description of reality, but a purely literary creation.

3. Shôhei Imamura, *The Ballad of Narayama*, 1983. The first adaptation for cinema by Keisuke Kinoshita was done in 1958.

4. Rereading these two wonderful books, ones that had been so important to me at different points in my life, would, a few months later, be the starting point for the book you are reading.

5. Maryse Condé, *What Is Africa to Me? Fragments of a True-to-Life Autobiography*, trans. Richard Philcox (Seagull Books, 2017), 196–97.

6. Even though it comes from a very different social location, a book by André Gorz comes to mind, *Letter to D*, which begins with these sentences: "You're 82 years old. You've shrunk six centimeters, you only weigh 45 kilos yet you're still beautiful, graceful and desirable. We've lived together now for 58 years and I love you more than ever." *Letter to D: A Love Story*, trans. Julie Rose (Polity, 2009), 1.

7. Yasushi Inoue, *Chronicle of My Mother*, trans. Jean Oda Moy (Kodansha International, 1982), 46, 49.

8. On femicide, see Christelle Taraud, ed., *Féminicides: Une histoire mondiale* (La Découverte, 2022).

9. Édouard Louis, *A Woman's Battles and Transformations*, trans. Tash Aw (Farrar, Straus and Giroux, 2022).

10. The expression "to sleep in separate rooms" [*faire chambre à part*] is often used to indicate that a couple is not getting along, is divided. Yet my parents were the perfect example of a divided couple—there was never a moment when they got along—for which it would have been impossible for them not to sleep in the same room. One reason was that the apartments they lived in (with their children) never had more than one, two, or maximum, three bedrooms, and so there was never one available for them to sleep separately; but the main reason was that it would simply have been unthinkable. It has to do with a norm that defines a couple as "under the same roof, in the same bed." I know as well that my parents had sexual relations for a long time: they had two children after me, and when we were living in a newly built housing project on the edge of the city, the units were so tiny and built out of such low-quality materials that you could hear everything from one room to the next and even from across the hall. Judging from the remarks that my mother would make, I understood that these relations did not provide them much in the way of pleasure.

11. Later, in 1979, in a song called "Le bilan" (The balance sheet), he would denounce the statement made by Georges Marchais, secretary general of the French Communist Party, declaring that the "balance sheet" of the socialist regime in the USSR was "overall positive."

12. Jean Ferrat, "Ma France," from the album *Ma France*, Barclay, 1969. When the album was released, this particular song was banned on French television.

13. Jean Ferrat, "Tu verras, tu seras bien," from the album *Ferrat 80*, Temey, 1980.

14. Yehoshua Kenaz, *The Way to the Cats*, trans. Dalya Bilu (Steerforth, 1991), 124.

15. Barney G. Glaser and Anselm L. Strauss, "The Ritual Drama of Mutual Pretense," in *The Awareness of Dying* (Aldine, 1965), 64–78.

16. For a discussion of this point, see Isabelle Mallon, "Entrer en maison de retraite: Rupture ou tournant biographique?," *Gérontologie et société* 30, no. 121 (2007): 251–64.

17. Samuel Beckett, *Molloy*, trans. Patrick Bowles in collaboration with the author, in *Three Novels by Samuel Beckett: "Molloy," "Malone Dies," "The Unnameable"* (Grove, 1965), 7.

18. In French, Coetzee's "Lies" ("Mensonges") is part of a volume called *L'abattoir de verre* (Seuil, 2018). "Lies" was published in English in the December 21, 2017, issue of *The New York Review of Books*.—Trans.

19. Bohumil Hrabal, *Harlequin's Millions*, trans. Stacey Knecht (Archipelago Books, 2014), 67.

20. Norbert Elias, *The Loneliness of the Dying*, trans. Edmund Jephcott (Continuum, 2001), 74.

21. Hrabal, *Harlequin's Millions*, 17.

22. Of course, the EHPAD's residents, my mother being a prime example, came from all over the region, but it's worth pointing out that Fismes is one of the poorest towns in the department of the Marne, and as one might therefore expect in this part of the country, this rural village with six thousand inhabitants votes massively for the extreme right. Marine Le Pen won 56 percent of the votes there in the second round of the 2017 presidential elections, as compared to Macron's 44 percent. In 2022 it was 62 percent to his 38 percent.

23. Hrabal, *Harlequin's Millions*, 76.

24. Didier Eribon, *Insult and the Making of the Gay Self*, trans. Michael Lucey (Duke University Press, 2004); and Didier Eribon, *Une morale du minoritaire: Variations sur un theme de Jean Genet* (Fayard, 2001).

25. Hrabal, *Harlequin's Millions*, 156.

26. Hrabal, *Harlequin's Millions*, 156–57.

27. On the difficulties a newcomer has in adapting to an institution's rules, and on the degree to which that adaptation necessarily involves a reconfiguration of all their habits, and even a transformation of their very person, the loss of a sense of autonomy, see Erving Goffman, *Asylums: Essays on the Social Situation of Mental Patients and Other Inmates* (Anchor Books, 1961).

28. See, for example, Gu Xiaogang's 2019 film, *Dwelling in the Fuchun Mountains*, which shows a group of children who would like to have their mother move into a retirement home until the wife of one of the sons agrees to take her in and to take care of her. See also, among many others, Yasushi Inoue's *Chronicle of My Mother*, mentioned earlier. There is also Annie Ernaux's *A Woman's Story*, or Hélène Cixous's *Mother Homer Is Dead* ...

29. On the working conditions of in-home care workers who care for senior citizens and others with restricted mobility, see the first few chapters of Anne-Sophie Pelletier, *EHPAD, une honte française* (Plon, 2019). The author goes so far as to speak of the "failure to provide assistance to people at risk" when discussing the state's scandalous failure to attend to the situation of these dependent people, delegating the responsibility to private firms, who view the situation as a "lucrative market" and a source of profits (94). See also the film by Ken Loach, *Sorry We Missed You* (2018), in which one of the two main characters (the woman, played by Debbie Honeywood) works in one of these exhausting and badly paid jobs. See also the 2020 film by Gilles Perret and François Ruffin, *Those Who Care* (*Debout les femmes!*).

30. On the concept of "territories of the self," see Erving Goffman, *Relations in Public: Microstudies of the Public Order* (Basic Books, 1971), 28–61.

31. The expression *peau de chagrin* comes from the title of a novel by Honoré de Balzac, in which a magical skin, the *peau de chagrin*, grants its possessor their wishes, but shrinks with every wish granted, until, with the disappearance of the skin, the possessor's life comes to an end.—Trans.

32. Hrabal, *Harlequin's Millions*, 279–80.

33. Annie Ernaux, *A Woman's Story*, trans. Tanya Leslie (Seven Stories, 1991), 78.

34. Christa Wolf, *In the Flesh*, trans. John S. Barrett (David R. Godine, 2005), 83.

35. Wolf, *In the Flesh*, 46–47.

36. Wolf, *In the Flesh*, 47–48.

37. I came to a better understanding of what my mother must have been experiencing when I read the pages in Zeruya Shalev's novel *The Remains of Love* in which the elderly mother, sick and bedridden, struggles with her dark thoughts: "the room … suddenly seems so vast to her, so spacious her eyes struggle to take it all in, has it really grown or is she the one who has shrunk? This is the smallest room in a minuscule apartment, but now as she is confined to her bed from morning to evening it seems its dimensions have expanded." *The Remains of Love*, trans. Philip Simpson (Bloomsbury, 2013), 349–50.

38. It is the word used by Anne-Sophie Pelletier. Having been an in-home care worker for a time, she then worked in an EHPAD (a privately owned one). The second part of her book (*EHPAD, une honte française*, cited earlier), which recounts in a concrete and detailed fashion her experience of this profession, is as painful to

read as is the first part, but it is also indispensable reading. It confronts us with the reality of these nursing homes, and once we have been exposed to that, we have no choice but to rise up and call for change. See also Hella Kherief, *Le scandale des EHPAD: Une aide-soignante dénonce le traitement indigne des personnes âgée* (Hugo–New Life, 2019).

39. *Les droits fondamentaux des personnes âgées accueillies en EHPAD* (Défenseur des droits, 2021), https://www.defenseurdesdroits.fr/rapport-les-droits-fondamentaux-des-personnes-agees-accueillies-en-ehpad-260.

40. *Suivi des recommandations du rapport sur les droits fondamentaux des personnes âgées accueillies en EHPAD* (Défenseur des droits, 2023), https://www.defenseurdes-droits.fr/rapport-suivi-des-recommandations-du-rapport-sur-les-droits-fondamentaux-des-personnes-agees-261.

41. See Victor Castanet, *Les fossoyeurs: Révélations sur le système qui maltraite nos aînés* (Fayard, 2022), which describes the situation in a private EHPAD near Paris where even meals for residents are rationed, while their families pay huge fortunes to lodge them there.

42. Goffman, *Asylums*, xiii.

43. The sickening contrast between the way a nursing home is portrayed in its publicity materials and what actually takes place there is taken up in the chapter titled "Belavista" in Julie Otsuka's novel *The Swimmers* (Knopf, 2022), where this management, this control, these restrictions, and ultimately this depersonalization are laid bare in a tragicomic mode. It is chilling to read. And it is hardly a dystopia: such is the reality of the situation once you agree to see it.

44. Georges Duby, *William Marshal: The Flower of Chivalry*, trans. Richard Howard (Pantheon Books, 1985), 3–26.

45. The difficulties in understanding such a situation, the fact that children's reactions are always out of sync with what is really happening to their parents, are shown clearly in Michael Haneke's film *Amour* (2012), in which the daughter of an elderly couple (Emmanuelle Riva and Jean-Louis Trintignant), played brilliantly by Isabelle Huppert, is slow to understand what is happening when the health of her mother, who has suffered a stroke, inexorably deteriorates.

46. See Thomas Desmidt, "Le syndrome de glissement," *La revue du practicien* 69, no. 1 (2019): 80–82. He attributes the formulation of this concept to a thesis written by Jean Carrié in 1956 on *Les modes de décès des vieillards à l'hospice* (The manners of death of the elderly in hospice), and then reviews all the critiques to which the

concept has been subjected, especially by psychiatrists, who claim it could simply mask other factors such as depression or delirium … I am not a doctor, but as far as the case of my mother is concerned, the concept seems to me to account more than adequately for what happened to her, thanks to the way in which it brings together a set of factors like despair, delirium, and depression.

47. Kenaz, *Way to the Cats*, 195.

48. Bertolt Brecht, "The Unseemly Old Lady," trans. Yvonne Kapp, in *The Collected Short Stories of Bertolt Brecht*, ed. John Willett and Ralph Manheim (Bloomsbury, 2015), 251, 253, 254.

49. Racine, *Phèdre*, act 1, scene 3.

50. Elias, *Loneliness of the Dying*, 89.

51. Or, more simply: Why should Max Brod have felt obliged to burn Kafka's manuscripts just because Kafka asked him to? Especially since we know that the degree of respect for requests like these can change over time: in the case of Foucault, the situation evolved from a strict rule of "no posthumous publications" in the years immediately following his death, to the posthumous publication of everything that could be found, from his courses to his notes for his courses, as well as, along the way, older texts that the author himself had left unpublished. (Myself, I favor this latter solution, but wonder why it should be necessary to put it off for twenty, thirty, or forty years?)

52. Duby, *William Marshal*, 5.

53. Philippe Ariès, *The Hour of Our Death*, trans. Helen Weaver (Knopf, 1981); and Philippe Ariès, *Western Attitudes Toward Death: From the Middle Ages to the Present*, trans. Patricia M. Ranum (Johns Hopkins University Press, 1975).

54. Michel Foucault, "Social Security," trans. Alan Sheridan, in *Politics, Philosophy, Culture: Interviews and Other Writings of Michel Foucault, 1977–1984*, ed. Lawrence D. Kritzman (Routledge, 1990), 177 (translation modified).

55. Albert Cohen, *Book of My Mother*, trans. Bella Cohen (Peter Owen, 1997), 118.

56. Imre Kertész, *L'ultime auberge* (Actes Sud, 2019), 127.

57. On friendship as a mode of life that sets itself apart from the family, see Geoffroy de Lagasnerie, 3: *Une aspiration au dehors* (Flammarion, 2023).

58. Marcel Mauss, "The Obligatory Expression of Feelings (Australian Oral Funerary Rituals)," trans. Alexander Jones, *Anthropological Quarterly* 82, no. 1 (2009): 297–303.

59. Pierre Bourdieu, "On the Family as a Realized Category," *Theory, Culture & Society* 13, no.3 (1996): 19–26.

60. Pierre Bourdieu, "The Biographical Illusion," trans. Yves Winkin and Wendy Leeds-Hurwitz, in *Identity: A Reader*, ed. Paul du Gay, Jessica Evans, and Peter Redman (Sage, 2004), 297–303.

61. Simone de Beauvoir, *Old Age*, trans. Patrick O'Brian (André Deutsch and Weidenfeld and Nicolson, 1972), 83.

62. Philip Roth, *Patrimony: A True Story* (Knopf Doubleday, 1996), 36.

63. Ernaux, *A Woman's Story*, 90.

64. Louis Aragon, *Le roman inachevé* (Gallimard, 1972), 177.

65. On the way in which parents experience and perceive the rising social trajectories of their children, see Adrien Naselli, *Et tes parents, ils font quoi? Enquête sur les transfuges de classe et leurs parents* (JC Lattès, 2021).

66. Hélène Cixous, *Mother Homer Is Dead*, trans. Peggy Kamuf (Edinburgh University Press, 2018). See also Hélène Cixous, *Osnabrück Station to Jerusalem*, trans. Peggy Kamuf (Fordham University Press, 2020); and Hélène Cixous and Cécile Wajsbrot, *Une autobiographie allemande* (Christian Bourgois, 2016).

67. Michel Tamine, *Le parler de Champagne* (Christine Bonneton, 2018).

68. Danilo Kiš, "The Encyclopedia of the Dead (A Whole Life)," in *The Encyclopedia of the Dead*, trans. Michael Henry Heim (Northwestern University Press, 1997), 42, 49, 54, 51, 64.

69. On the notions of "linguistic market" and of "legitimate language," see Pierre Bourdieu, "The Economy of Linguistic Exchanges," part 1 in *Language and Symbolic Power*, ed. John B. Thompson, trans. Gino Raymond and Matthew Adamson (Harvard University Press, 1991).

70. We could also mention the indignation of the "learned ladies" in Molière's play of the same title (highly misogynistic in its own right), in their dealings with the servant, Martine, whom they fire because she has committed the "unpardonable

crime" of offending good grammar, the laws of language, and the rules of correct speech (act 2, scenes 6 and 7). It is worth pointing out that the male character who comes to the defense of the servant and her way of speaking gives as the reason for his indulgence that her French mistakes are unimportant as long as she cooks well. The class relationship is thus the same in both cases.

71. Lynsey Hanley, *Respectable: The Experience of Class* (Allen Lane, 2016), 129. A study of accents in the UK shows, for example, that 44 percent of students from the north of England fear, both before they enter university and once they are there, that their working-class accent will negatively affect their future success and their professional career. Nearly 30 percent of managers and executives from the working classes confirm that they have been made fun of in professional circumstances because of their accent. This means that throughout their whole life, the hierarchization of accents poses a problem for those who speak with an "inferior" accent once they have left the geographic and social space where those accents are widespread. The authors of the study emphasize both the objective evidence of discrimination produced by the stratification of accents and the feelings of fear and anxiety that are the result of this. "A hierarchy of accent prestige has been entrenched in the United Kingdom for centuries, with Received Pronunciation (sometimes known as 'Queen's English' or 'BBC English') the dominant accent in positions of authority across the media, politics, the civil service, courtrooms, and the corporate sector. This is despite less than 10% of the population estimated to have this accent, almost exclusively from higher socio-economic backgrounds." Erez Levon, Devyani Sharma, and Christian Ilbury, *Speaking Up: Accents and Social Mobility* (Sutton Trust, 2022).

72. Cohen, *Book of My Mother*, 28, 70.

73. Cohen, *Book of My Mother*, 61.

74. Cohen, *Book of My Mother*, 120.

75. Obviously this rudimentary kind racism is not to be found only in the working classes.

76. Henry Louis Gates Jr., *Colored People* (Vintage Books, 1995), 22.

77. Gates, *Colored People*, 150.

78. Didier Eribon, *La société comme verdict: Classes, identités, trajectoires* (Fayard, 2013).

79. A racist term for immigrants from North Africa.—Trans.

80. Gates, *Colored People*, 202, 206–7.

81. *Simple Passion* (2020), a film by Danielle Arbid, adapted from Annie Ernaux's novel of the same title. Ernaux's character is played by Laetitia Dosch.

82. An internet search sends me to the Harlequin Books site. (How did I not think of that earlier?) I thus find on my computer screen volumes identical to the ones my mother was reading, with the same covers (on which the two people are always young and beautiful, and always white). I am forced to admit that my interest in reading a few of them is not strong enough to convince me to order any of them online.

83. Karl Marx and Friedrich Engels, *Le syndicalisme*, trans. Roger Dangeville, 2 vols. (Maspero, 1972).

84. Pierre Bourdieu, *On Television*, trans. Priscilla Parkhurst Ferguson (New Press, 1998), 17; and Pierre Bourdieu, "*Sur la television*," *suivi de* "*L'emprise du journalism*" (Liber–Raisons d'Agir, 1996), 16.

85. See Marcel Caille, *L'assassin était chez Citroën* (Sociales, 1978).

86. I described this scene in "Qui est 'je': Genèse, enjeux et reception de l'auto-analyse," in Didier Eribon, *Principes d'une pensée critique* (Fayard, 2016), 83–85.

87. Patrick Chamoiseau, *La matière de l'absence* (Seuil, 2016), 120.

88. Norbert Elias, *The Civilizing Process*, 2 vols. (Blackwell, 1969–82). In French: *Sur le processus de civilization*, trans. Pierre Kamnitzer, 2 vols. (Calmann-Lévy, 1973–75).

89. Didier Eribon, *Michel Foucault*, trans. Betsy Wing (Harvard University Press, 1991), ix. In Jephcott's translation: "Death hides no secret. It opens no door. It is the end of a person. What survives is what he or she has given to other people, what stays in their memory." Elias, *Loneliness of the Dying*, 67.

90. Elias, *Loneliness of the Dying*, 67, 69.

91. Elias, *Loneliness of the Dying*, 72 (italics in the original), 70, 69.

92. Simone de Beauvoir, "The Age of Discretion," in *The Woman Destroyed*, trans. Patrick O'Brian (G. P. Putnam's Sons, 1969), 14.

93. Simone de Beauvoir, *All Said and Done*, trans. Patrick O'Brian (G. P. Putnam's Sons, 1974), 130–31 (translation modified).

94. Simone de Beauvoir, *The Second Sex*, trans. Constance Borde and Sheila Malovany-Chevallier (Vintage Books, 2011), 17.

95. Maurice Merleau-Ponty, *Phenomenology of Perception*, trans. Colin Smith (Routledge & Kegan Paul, 1962).

96. Benedict de Spinoza, "*On the Improvement of the Understanding*," "*The Ethics*," *Correspondence*, trans. R. H. M. Elwes (Dover, 1955), 12.

97. The first English translation was made from an abridged edition and published in 1965 under the title *Madness and Civilization: A History of Insanity in the Age of Reason*.—Trans.

98. Michel Foucault, *History of Madness*, ed. Jean Khalfa, trans. Jonathan Murphy and Jean Khalfa (Routledge, 2006), xxviii; and Beauvoir, *Old Age*, 2.

99. A "history of the present," an "ethnology of our own culture," "archaeology," and "genealogy" are, of course, all terms Foucault used at different moments in his work.

100. René Descartes, *"Meditations on First Philosophy," with Selections from the Objections and Replies*, trans. John Cottingham, rev. ed. (Cambridge University Press, 1996), 13.

101. Foucault, *History of Madness*, 101, xvii; and *Michel Foucault, Mental Illness and Psychology*, trans. Alan Sheridan (University of California Press, 1987), 67.

102. Foucault, *History of Madness*, 250. Foucault's structuralism is inspired by that of Georges Dumézil. It consists in showing how one finds the same organizing structure at different levels of a society and a culture. I analyzed these texts in the third part of *Insult and the Making of the Gay Self*, called "Michel Foucault's Heterotopias," notably in the chapter called "Homosexuality and Unreason" (264–73).

103. Foucault, *History of Madness*, 207 (translation modified).

104. Foucault, *History of Madness*, 542.

105. Jean Améry, *On Aging: Revolt and Resignation*, trans. John D. Barlow (Indiana University Press, 1994).

106. Beauvoir, *All Said and Done*, 130.

107. Beauvoir, *The Second Sex*, 8–9.

108. Simone de Beauvoir, *La vieillesse* (Gallimard, 1970), copy from the back cover.

109. These movements have been the object of a number of studies. Let me mention by way of example Jean-Philippe Viriot Durandal, *Le pouvoir gris: Sociologie des groupes de pression de retraités* (Presses universitaires de France, 2003); and, for Switzerland, Alexandre Lambelet, *Des âgés en AG: Sociologie des organisations de défense des retraités* (Antipodes, 2014).

110. Beauvoir, *Old Age*, 85.

111. Beauvoir, *Old Age*, 3, 543, 541, 3 (translations slightly modified). One can find the same kind of economism in Foucault when he explains the exclusion of "unreason" as a pushing aside of the "idle" at a moment when a new "sensibility" linked to bourgeois morality is being established.

112. Jean-Paul Sartre, "Simone de Beauvoir Interviews Sartre," in *Life/Situations: Essays Written and Spoken*, trans. Paul Auster and Lydia Davis (Pantheon Books, 1977), 93–108.

113. Beauvoir, *Old Age*, 543.

114. See Pierre Bourdieu, In *Other Words: Essays Towards a Reflexive Sociology*, trans. Matthew Adamson (Stanford University Press, 1990), 18, 75, 129, 132, 134; and Pierre Bourdieu, "Formes d'action politique et modes d'existence des groupes," in *Propos sur le champ politique* (Presse universitaires de Lyon, 2000), 80–88.

ALLEN LANE
an imprint of
PENGUIN BOOKS

Also Published

C. Thi Nguyen, *The Score: How to Stop Playing Someone Else's Game*

Sven Beckert, *Capitalism: A Global History*

Maria Alyokhina, *Political Girl: Life and Fate in Russia*

Branko Milanović, *The Great Global Transformation: National Market Liberalism in a Multipolar World*

Paul McCartney, *Wings: The Story of a Band on the Run*

Graham Harman, *Waves and Stones: On the Ultimate Nature of Reality*

Jonathan C. Slaght, *Tigers Between Empires: The Journey to Save the Siberian Tiger from Extinction*

Paul Gillingham, *Mexico: A History*

César A. Hidalgo, *The Infinite Alphabet: And the Laws of Knowledge*

Hu Anyan, *I Deliver Parcels in Beijing: On Making a Living*

Sudhir Hazareesingh, *Daring to be Free: Rebellion and Resistance of the Enslaved in the Atlantic World*

Hans Ulrich Obrist, *Life in Progress*

Richard H. Thaler and Alex O. Imas, *The Winner's Curse: Behavioral Economics Anomalies Then and Now*

Vlatko Vedral, *Portals to a New Reality: Five Experiments to Unlock the Future of Physics*

Robin Holloway, *Music's Odyssey: An Invitation to Western Classical Music*

Andrew Ross Sorkin, *1929: The Inside Story of The Greatest Crash in Wall Street History*

Andrew Graham-Dixon, *Vermeer: A Life Lost and Found*

Serhii Plokhy, *The Nuclear Age: An Epic Race for Arms, Power and Survival*

Charles Moore, *Margaret Thatcher: The Authorized Biography: Single-volume Centenary Edition*

Steven Pinker, *When Everyone Knows That Everyone Knows...: Common Knowledge and the Science of Harmony, Hypocrisy and Outrage*

Malcolm Gaskill, *The Glass Mountain: Escape and Discovery in Wartime Italy*

Mark Mazower, *On Antisemitism: A Word in History*

Sara Ahmed, *No Is Not a Lonely Utterance: The Art and Activism of Complaining*

Catherine Clarke, *A History of England in 25 Poems*

Carlo Rovelli, *Seven Brief Lessons on Physics*

Lea Ypi, *Indignity: A Life Reimagined*

Christopher Clark, *A Scandal in Königsberg*

Clare Jackson, *The Mirror of Great Britain: A Life of James VI & I*

ALLEN LANE
an imprint of
PENGUIN BOOKS

Also Published

C. Thi Nguyen, *The Score: How to Stop Playing Someone Else's Game*

Sven Beckert, *Capitalism: A Global History*

Maria Alyokhina, *Political Girl: Life and Fate in Russia*

Branko Milanović, *The Great Global Transformation: National Market Liberalism in a Multipolar World*

Paul McCartney, *Wings: The Story of a Band on the Run*

Graham Harman, *Waves and Stones: On the Ultimate Nature of Reality*

Jonathan C. Slaght, *Tigers Between Empires: The Journey to Save the Siberian Tiger from Extinction*

Paul Gillingham, *Mexico: A History*

César A. Hidalgo, *The Infinite Alphabet: And the Laws of Knowledge*

Hu Anyan, *I Deliver Parcels in Beijing: On Making a Living*

Sudhir Hazareesingh, *Daring to be Free: Rebellion and Resistance of the Enslaved in the Atlantic World*

Hans Ulrich Obrist, *Life in Progress*

Richard H. Thaler and Alex O. Imas, *The Winner's Curse: Behavioral Economics Anomalies Then and Now*

Vlatko Vedral, *Portals to a New Reality: Five Experiments to Unlock the Future of Physics*

Robin Holloway, *Music's Odyssey: An Invitation to Western Classical Music*

Andrew Ross Sorkin, *1929: The Inside Story of The Greatest Crash in Wall Street History*

Andrew Graham-Dixon, *Vermeer: A Life Lost and Found*

Serhii Plokhy, *The Nuclear Age: An Epic Race for Arms, Power and Survival*

Charles Moore, *Margaret Thatcher: The Authorized Biography: Single-volume Centenary Edition*

Steven Pinker, *When Everyone Knows That Everyone Knows...: Common Knowledge and the Science of Harmony, Hypocrisy and Outrage*

Malcolm Gaskill, *The Glass Mountain: Escape and Discovery in Wartime Italy*

Mark Mazower, *On Antisemitism: A Word in History*

Sara Ahmed, *No Is Not a Lonely Utterance: The Art and Activism of Complaining*

Catherine Clarke, *A History of England in 25 Poems*

Carlo Rovelli, *Seven Brief Lessons on Physics*

Lea Ypi, *Indignity: A Life Reimagined*

Christopher Clark, *A Scandal in Königsberg*

Clare Jackson, *The Mirror of Great Britain: A Life of James VI & I*

ALLEN LANE
an imprint of
PENGUIN BOOKS

Also Published

C. Thi Nguyen, *The Score: How to Stop Playing Someone Else's Game*

Sven Beckert, *Capitalism: A Global History*

Maria Alyokhina, *Political Girl: Life and Fate in Russia*

Branko Milanović, *The Great Global Transformation: National Market Liberalism in a Multipolar World*

Paul McCartney, *Wings: The Story of a Band on the Run*

Graham Harman, *Waves and Stones: On the Ultimate Nature of Reality*

Jonathan C. Slaght, *Tigers Between Empires: The Journey to Save the Siberian Tiger from Extinction*

Paul Gillingham, *Mexico: A History*

César A. Hidalgo, *The Infinite Alphabet: And the Laws of Knowledge*

Hu Anyan, *I Deliver Parcels in Beijing: On Making a Living*

Sudhir Hazareesingh, *Daring to be Free: Rebellion and Resistance of the Enslaved in the Atlantic World*

Hans Ulrich Obrist, *Life in Progress*

Richard H. Thaler and Alex O. Imas, *The Winner's Curse: Behavioral Economics Anomalies Then and Now*

Vlatko Vedral, *Portals to a New Reality: Five Experiments to Unlock the Future of Physics*

Robin Holloway, *Music's Odyssey: An Invitation to Western Classical Music*

Andrew Ross Sorkin, *1929: The Inside Story of The Greatest Crash in Wall Street History*

Andrew Graham-Dixon, *Vermeer: A Life Lost and Found*

Serhii Plokhy, *The Nuclear Age: An Epic Race for Arms, Power and Survival*

Charles Moore, *Margaret Thatcher: The Authorized Biography: Single-volume Centenary Edition*

Steven Pinker, *When Everyone Knows That Everyone Knows...: Common Knowledge and the Science of Harmony, Hypocrisy and Outrage*

Malcolm Gaskill, *The Glass Mountain: Escape and Discovery in Wartime Italy*

Mark Mazower, *On Antisemitism: A Word in History*

Sara Ahmed, *No Is Not a Lonely Utterance: The Art and Activism of Complaining*

Catherine Clarke, *A History of England in 25 Poems*

Carlo Rovelli, *Seven Brief Lessons on Physics*

Lea Ypi, *Indignity: A Life Reimagined*

Christopher Clark, *A Scandal in Königsberg*

Clare Jackson, *The Mirror of Great Britain: A Life of James VI & I*